Transition Leadership

Catherine Hayes

Transition Leadership

Navigating the Complexities
of Organisational Change

 Springer

Catherine Hayes
Transition Dynamics, London, UK

ISBN 978-3-030-42789-4   ISBN 978-3-030-42787-0   (eBook)
https://doi.org/10.1007/978-3-030-42787-0

This Springer imprint is published by the registered company Springer Nature Switzerland AG
The registered company address is: Gewerbestrasse 11, 6330 Cham, Switzerland

This text is dedicated to all leaders and change professionals who are faced with the task of supporting organisations to navigate the multifaceted dynamics of today's continuously changing environments.

Preface

This book is the result of an evolving journey of discoveries based on 30 years of organisational development practice and applied research. The content has been derived through weaving Buddhist philosophy and clinical and business psychology practices whilst working in partnership with executives, leaders and change professionals across a range of different industries.

Supporting individuals, teams and organisations to navigate transitions has evolved into becoming a vocational life purpose. My curiosity and passion for transitions began in 1990, experiencing one organisational change project fail after another. I watched leaders with 20-year track records of success stumble and fall whilst trying to navigate transformation challenges. My observations revealed how many resources were being wasted, as leaders unintentionally derailed their careers and the broader challenging impact this had on the functioning of their organisations.

The questions that provoked curiosity and intrigue in 1990 were: What makes the wheels fall off well thought through transformation strategies when talented, intelligent leaders try to implement them? What happens in the space between ideas and implementation that seems so complicated, messy and challenging that causes a great deal of suffering for organisations?

Switching a technology career for an organisation development career in the early 1990s, I realised that the challenges organisations were facing were all related to people, unintentionally getting in their own ways. After studying two training and development and British Psychological Society qualifications, I discovered that the methods and best practices that I was taught at the time were overly simplistic. At the time, the approaches and theories that I was studying and trying to put into practice were out of alignment with what I was experiencing in reality. Trying to understand so many unknowns, I began a search to see if I could shine more light into the 'why, what and how' of organisational change.

My transition exploration journey began with neuro linguistic programming (NLP) whilst it was useful for seeing repeating patterns; the question I couldn't answer was 'why'. Why do functional and dysfunctional patterns in thinking and behaviour occur, and what causes them?

The next stops on the journey of discovery were Gestalt, Transaction Analysis and Humanistic psychologies. These were closely followed by an MSc in Change Agent Skills and Strategies, where I explored a range of action research methods and approaches. At the time, responsible for an infrastructure organisation development agenda in Morgan Stanley Investment Bank, I began conducting participatory action research projects with colleagues. We uncovered many causes to organisational transformation challenges, and yet, I still had many unknown questions related to the 'why' that I couldn't answer.

Integrating 10 years of research with business development and transformation experiences, I began to create transition leadership methods and approaches – supporting leaders and line managers to develop new capabilities whilst practically implementing their change agendas. Our efforts evolved into creating a development practice that at the time we labelled as 'developing whilst delivering'.

In 2004, I was presented with an exciting opportunity to create a new global OD function for Schroders asset management, and I utilised my research and development approaches to support leaders to solve a range of complex business challenges. As part of the process of designing and implementing a new global OD agenda, I became interested in systemic group development. My curiosities opened up a new development pathway, where I incorporated Systems-Centred therapy approaches into my organisational practice.

In 2007, my applied transition research and development approach drew interest from Cass Business School, and I was invited to join the visiting faculty as a transition specialist practitioner. In partnership with academic and practitioner colleagues, we formed a centre to support change practitioners to develop capabilities to work with transitions. Part of the programme was to design and facilitate the Transition Leadership Series for Executive MBA students. This project coincided with switching the direction of my career into setting up a transition consulting practice.

At the time, I had formed the belief that what organisations lacked was transition leadership capabilities. This belief was shattered, as I began working with organisations across different industry sectors. What I had overlooked in my own practice was institutional knowledge. As a transition consultant, I uncovered another core challenge, that leaders did not understand the operational functioning of their organisations. With the lack of insight into operational functioning combined with applying procedural change methods, leaders unintentionally got in their own ways. The outcomes resembled as though they were trying to drive blindfolded with the brakes on. In practice, leaders made their journeys of navigating transitions more complicated and messy than they needed to be.

My discoveries evoked a new curiosity that related to the Buddhist concept of impermanence, a philosophical concept of life being a process of continuous change that is a given in Buddhist culture. It was a philosophical concept that seemed to be somewhat non-existent in our control-orientated Western mind-set. Intrigued to understand the constructs and underlying functioning of the Western mind-set, I began what became a 4-year journey of studying Buddhist psychology and Core Process Psychotherapy.

Applying my learning to both clinical and organisatioral environments, I finally got to the bottom of my questions. The reason why organisations struggled with embracing change was based on their responses to not knowing in many different contexts. Leaders could not articulate how their organisat on functioned. They also didn't understand the nature of transitions and how to work with the various facets of ambiguity and complexity that transitional processes evoke. It was a challenge that applied to individuals, teams and whole organisations. As a result, leaders and their workforces did not know how to navigate successful transitions. In practice, leaders struggled to lead themselves through their transition challenges, let alone support others or their organisations to do the same. This discovery opened up another pathway for my organisational practice. Recogn sing that leaders needed support to understand the functioning of their organisations, in 2008, I began developing diagnostic tools and methods to complement the transition leadership approach.

The content of this book is not just something that I support organisations and executive MBA students to develop; it has evolved into a transformation approach that is at the core of my consulting practice today. Transition leadership has become a transformation practice that supports organisations to build sustainable capabilities and methods for working with a wide range of transition-related challenges.

My hope is that as you read and engage with the content of what I have discovered and integrated into my practice, the outcomes will become resources to inform and support your own transition and development journeys.

London, UK   Catherine Hayes

Acknowledgments

I would like to thank all the organisational leaders who have contributed to the transition research and practices over the years; the dedicated work and support of Maura and Franklyn Sills that helped me to find the final pieces to complete the jigsaw on the challenges of our Western mind-set; my husband, friends and colleagues for their encouragement to translate my transition practice into writing; and Springer Publishing for their support in making this book become a reality.

About This Book

This textbook provides insights and effective practices for leading and working with the complex dynamics of transitions in organisations. It consists of three parts:

Part I: Insights into Transitions

Part I unveils the complex dimensions of transitions and the unseen challenges that leaders face whilst trying to navigate and work with organisational transformations.

Chapter 1, Introduction, sets the scene for the whole textbook, outlining the key principle challenges that leaders are faced with and the importance of taking an integrated approach to organisational change.

Chapter 2, Transition Perspectives, explores the foundations for why we, as human beings, leaders and organisations, find navigating transitions challenging. This chapter explains the concept of Transition Blindness and why it has become a common leadership ailment. It provides an overview of the existing literature on transitions and why the concept of change management is no longer fit for the purpose of navigating the complexities of change in today's organisations.

Chapter 3, Territories of Transitions, shines light into the dynamics of the transitional space, introducing the transition cycle, a framework for understanding the complexities and unseen aspects that influence all transitional journeys. This chapter highlights the essential principles that honouring and working with complexity are core enablers of leading effective transformation processes. It explains the fundamental principles that when leaders can see and know the complex territories of the transitional space, they can develop approaches for working with them and support their organisations to do the same.

Chapter 4, The Impact of Transitions, provides insights into approaches for recognising, understanding and working with ambiguity, a natural inherent aspect present in all transitional processes. This chapter reveals how the psychological constructs of the Western mind-set contribute to fear-based behaviours that unintentionally make the processes of navigating change challenging and stressful experiences. It reveals the foundations for what has generally become termed as 'resistance to change and politics' in organisations; providing practical insights for learning how to recognise the symptoms in individuals, teams and organisational environments as they appear; and introducing the concept of the importance of knowing the nature of the self-self relationship as a core transition leadership competency.

Part II: Transition Leadership

Part II explores the practice of transition leadership. It describes the core principles of a practice that supports individuals, teams and organisations to navigate and work with the dimensions of continuously changing environments.

Chapter 5, Self-Insight, focuses on deepening an insight into the principle of knowing the self in a transition leadership context. This chapter explores why drawing awareness to unseen and overlooked aspects of human beings is a resource for supporting effective transition leadership practices. It reveals practical approaches for gaining knowledge and insight into factors that influence and inform what leaders do and how they approach their leadership agendas. It explores the different types of transitions that inform the evolution of a successful leadership career path and illuminating how core capabilities influence and inform patterns in the way that leaders approach and work with their transitional challenges.

Chapter 6, Team Transitions, illustrates the practices for facilitating transitional stages of team development and revealing the core leadership approaches that contribute to creating, facilitating and supporting the development of productive high-performing teams. It shares practical approaches derived from 15 years of research into the dynamics of high and low-performing teams, across a range of different industries.

Chapter 7, Creating Supportive Environments, explains why supportive environments are the core foundations and enablers for individuals, teams and organisations to navigate and work with the complexities of transitions. This chapter presents practical approaches for how to create contexts of safety and developing mutuality. It illustrates key aspects that reduce the risks of complexity and ambiguity overwhelm to enable leaders to create supportive contexts that facilitate creativity and innovation. It also explores core practices that enable organisations to utilise complexity and ambiguity to create competitive advantages in today's environments.

Chapter 8, Transition Practices, focuses on unveiling the factors that contribute to unnecessary complexity and ambiguity, exploring key business risk mitigation practices and approaches that support individuals, teams and organisations to navigate the different territories of the transitional space.

Part III: Transition Inquiry Practices

Whether it is individuals, teams or organisations, leading and facilitating any type of transitional process will require some aspect of inquiry. Presented in an applied practitioner context, Part III focuses on approaches and methods for facilitating effective organisational and self-inquiry processes.

Chapter 9, Inquiry in Organisations, shows how inquiry outcomes can provide valuable insights to support the effective design, implementation and facilitation of transition strategies. This chapter focuses on resourceful practices for inquiring with others, utilising a focused case study to provide insight into how a range of different approaches and methods can support a wide variety of organisational transitions.

Chapter 10, Conducting Self-Inquiry, the practice of self-inquiry is at the heart of leading successful transitions. Self-inquiry is based on the core principle that having insight into the different facets of self-self relationships provides resources to support the effectiveness of transition leadership practices. This chapter outlines the methods and approaches that facilitate effective self-inquiry practices, providing practical resources for gaining access to patterns that contribute to the nature of the relationships that leaders have with complex territories of their transition experiences.

Contents

List of Figures

List of Tables

List of Case Studies

Part III: Transition Inquiry Practices

About the Author

Catherine Hayes is an Organisation Development, Culture Transformation and Transition Leadership specialist with 30 years' experience of improving operational and business performance through systemic problem-solving, designing, leading and facilitating organisation-wide transformation programmes. Following two Executive Organisation Development roles in the Financial Services, she transitioned into consulting in 2007, where she has worked across a broad range of industry sectors.

Working in partnership with CEOs, boards and executive teams, Catherine supports organisations to understand and navigate complex, development and transformation challenges to deliver tangible results. Her passion and vocational purpose are supporting leaders and their organisations to embed transition leadership capabilities into their operational functioning and enabling leaders to utilise and replicate factors of success to enhance organisational effectiveness and create sustainable operational and business performance.

Combining her practice and applied research with Buddhist philosophy and business and clinical psychology, Catherine has created transition diagnostic analytics and tools that support insight into the complex operational functioning of organisations. She utilises her transition leadership methodology and development approach to enable leaders and their workforces to acquire transition capabilities whilst implementing their transformation agendas. She also runs the Transition Leadership Series for Executive MBAs at Cass Business School.

Chapter 1
Introduction

Introduction

In today's global business world, navigating and working with the complexities of continuous change has become the norm. Fuelled by the advancements in technology, successfully navigating and working with the inherent complexities of organisational change has become an essential leadership requirement. This core leadership task involves working with many interdependent changes and transformation processes, projects and programmes all happening simultaneously, over the short and longer term. The driving force is the need to go faster, to sustain competitive advantage in a continuously evolving environment.

This interdependent approach to organisational change requires multiple transitions. Transitions are often led without insight into the impacts of operational and human functioning. Leaders find themselves grappling with a multitude of facets, within both themselves and the functioning of their organisations that they have to take into account to achieve desired outcomes.

The tendency for organisations today is to focus on the more tangible technical and structural aspects like technology, processes and systems. The common practice is to utilise structured methodologies in an attempt to manage the complex dynamics of change to drive and achieve successful outcomes. Frequently overlooked is the basic principle that it is human responses and relationships with transitional processes that can derail progress, not just the methodology and or technical aspects.

Admittedly the use of Artificial Intelligence (AI) is gaining a rapid pace in organisations, business and society. Despite AI's progress, organisations cannot yet exist without the effective functioning of their people, a basic principle that is often unseen. If we take people out of organisations, all that's left are fixed assets. Robotics and computers still have a way to go to replace the requirements for effective human functioning in organisations.

Increasing demands are being placed on leaders and line managers to successfully implement complex change programmes to meet operational and regulatory

© Springer Nature Switzerland AG 2020
C. Hayes, *Transition Leadership*, https://doi.org/10.1007/978-3-030-42787-0_1

requirements while balancing and maintaining shareholder value. One way that organisations are attempting to overcome this challenge is to engage large consulting organisations to design their change programmes. They then become disappointed, demotivated and often overwhelmed, when the frameworks and 55-page manuals that they have paid vast sums of money for do not quite match perceived reality.

Leaders find it difficult to grapple with the requirements and practical realities of the 'how to' navigate the multifaceted processes of transitions to translate strategies into successful outcomes. The ideas, methods and approaches for successful implementation seem intellectually achievable at the outset. And yet, a different story emerges when they attempt to implement strategies. Even with a road map, organisations and leaders find it challenging to navigate their way through the complexities of transitions to deliver effective transformations. There is also the additional factor that an objectively designed map may not be fit for purpose when it comes to trying to translate it into practical application.

Another aspect that compounds these challenges is that traditional transformation skills and methods of facilitating organisational change have been built on a different world paradigm. The term 'change management' creates the impression that somehow change can be controlled and contained, a term that facilitates the expectations of certainty. Leaders of today have underestimated and overlooked the capabilities and skills they need to successfully navigate their transitional challenges. The general oversight is how many facets, that leaders both within themselves and their organisations are required to take into account, to achieve desired outcomes. The impact is that they get in their own ways and unintentionally derail their change and transformation agendas.

Facilitating successful transitions in organisations has become an essential leadership requirement, and yet, leaders are continuously challenged to work with the multifaceted complexities of the transitional space. Leaders struggle to hold the different responses to uncertainty, competing tensions and related responses to ambiguity that are generated while stepping from what is known into an unknown future.

An Integrated Approach

While delivering on tangible outputs is essential, unfortunately, many organisational transformation programmes are failing to realise their full potential, wasting valuable financial and human resources. The primary reason is that leaders and organisations don't know what they don't know about how to navigate environments of continuous change. What I have discovered over the years is that successfully navigating organisational change in today's environment requires the integration of three key factors:

1. *Operational Functioning* – insight into how the organisation operates. Particularly how a combination of mind-sets and capabilities combined with preferences and motivations influence the performance and culture or organisations.
2. *Transitional Space* – understanding of the complex dimensions and dynamics that transitions evoke and the capabilities to work with them.
3. *Leadership Practices* – core skills, knowledge and approaches for working with environments of continuous change (Fig. 1.1).

My experience is that these three factors apply to individuals, teams and organisations as a whole. The focus of this book is to shine light into the transitional space and share the core leadership practices that facilitate successful transformations. Complex organisational leadership aspects that are broadly accepted in principle and at the same time, something that in practice are not straightforward tasks. This book provides depth of insight into the hidden dimensions of the transitional space, illuminating why transitions are challenging, what to do with them and how to work with them. The intent is to fill in gaps of the existing organisational change literature and explore new concepts of transitions.

This book includes practical approaches for working with the complex challenges that transitions evoke. The content has been designed to be a resource for

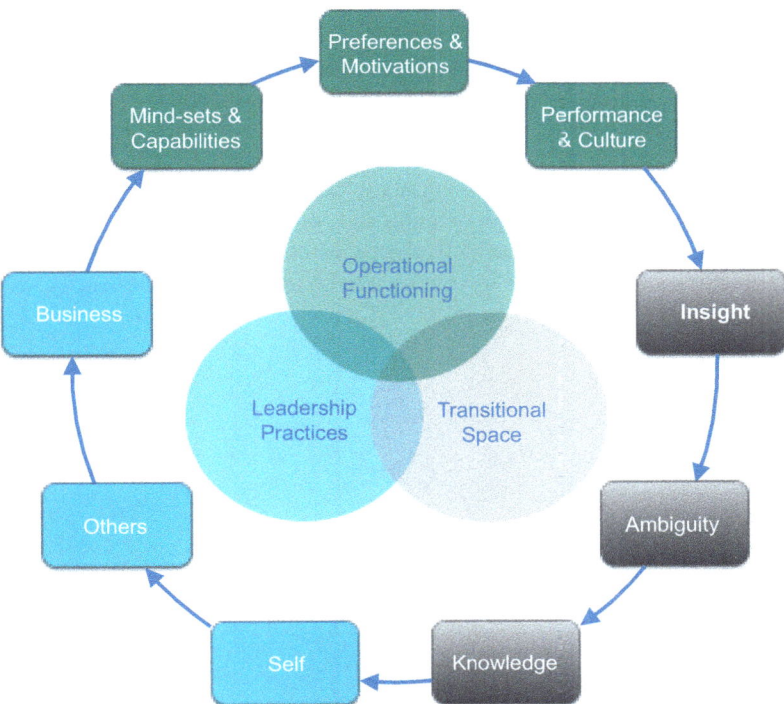

Fig. 1.1 An integrated approach to organisational change

supporting change leaders to gain insights into approaches for creating sustainable transition capabilities in their organisations. Sustainable practices for leading and effectively work with the on-going task of navigating the different territories of continuous change that organisations face in our world of today and tomorrow.

Invitation for Readers

The philosophy that underpins this book is that *it is difficult to lead others through transitions if we cannot lead ourselves.* Knowing how we as change leaders respond and relate to transitions is the key to unlocking the door and providing support for others and ultimately, organisations. Reflecting on my own personal insights and supporting the developmental experiences of organisations, I have found that leaders of today tend to have applied learning preferences. We gain the most from learning and developing new capabilities by applying concepts and perspectives to the practical realities of our own experiences. As a practitioner-researcher, I find new theories and perspectives intriguing. Theories are even more useful when I can apply them to inform my world experiences, acquire knowledge and facilitate the development of new capabilities and skills.

The invitation to you as a reader is to compare and contrast the content of this book with your own transition experiences. To explore how the concepts and approaches for working with transitions contained in this book are similar and different to those of your closest relationships, colleagues and/or the teams that you may be leading and working within. Plus, how might these concepts and approaches apply to your experiences of organisations as a whole?

Each chapter focuses on exploring a key transition-related topic, the relevance and importance to the leadership agenda and organisational effectiveness. A self-inquiry section at the end of each chapter provides resources for supporting practical application of the concepts to your own lived transitional experiences.

Part I
Insights into Transitions

Part I provides insights into the dynamics of transitions. Chapters 2, 3 and 4 focus on exploring the complex dimensions of transitions and the unseen challenges that leaders face while trying to work with the dynamics of individual, team and organisational transformation agendas. Multifaceted aspects that when overlooked can cause leaders and their organisations to unknowingly and unintentionally get in the way of their abilities to navigate change to deliver effective outcomes in today's environment.

Chapter 2
Transition Perspectives

Introduction

One of the many learnings from my organisational practice has been the importance of understanding context. I find that it is challenging to explore a concept without having insight into the broader context that it resides within. This chapter highlights why leaders and their organisations find the process of navigating the dynamics of change complex and challenging. It begins with the concept of transition blindness, and how the factors of oversimplification, haste and impatience that are prominent in our society today contribute to its impact, and why it has become a common leadership and organisation ailment. We then explore literature on transitions that inform current change leadership practices. These combined perspectives unveil how the concept of change management is built on the primary needs for simplicity and control. The core principles of a historical Western frame-of-reference honed over many decades, which unfortunately now is no longer fit for purpose for successfully navigating the complexities of change in today's organisations.

Transition Blindness

One of the most common challenges I observe organisations facing today is that they underestimate, overlook and often avoid the transitional space. As leaders focus on achieving results, being compliant with regulations or laws and organisational change agendas, they have a tendency to launch from intention straight into implementation. The impact is that leaders and their organisations suffer from the symptoms of transition blindness (Fig. 2.1).

© Springer Nature Switzerland AG 2020
C. Hayes, *Transition Leadership*, https://doi.org/10.1007/978-3-030-42787-0_2

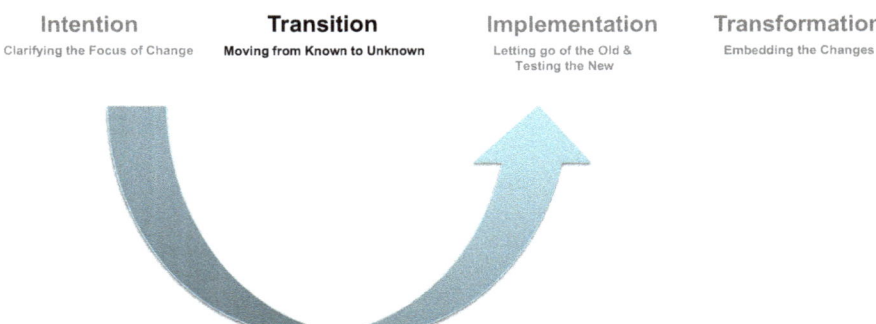

| Intention | **Transition** | Implementation | Transformation |
| Clarifying the Focus of Change | **Moving from Known to Unknown** | Letting go of the Old & Testing the New | Embedding the Changes |

Fig. 2.1 Transition blindness in practice

Transition Blindness Key Symptoms

Several factors contribute to the condition of Transition Blindness:

Oversimplification While navigating the complexities of their change agendas, organisations have a tendency to lean towards simplistic terms. Unfortunately, an unseen and unintentional impact of oversimplification is that it can facilitate tunnel vision. Change and transformation programmes are often given labels, like technology, process, people, regulatory, law, risk, compliance. The impact is that the utilisation of simplistic labels facilitates a dedicated focus for execution and delivery. The outcome results in a narrowly focused lens that leaders use to direct their attention and consolidate the impact of their efforts. The practical impact is what leaders look for is what they see. Leaders then find themselves surprised when something they hadn't seen or incorporated derails the progress or success of their change projects and transformation agendas.

Haste Despite the best intentions of wanting to achieve positive outcomes, the focus to achieve results takes centre stage. In a rush to achieve, deliver tangible outcomes and show practical results, leaders can often be reluctant to invest time and effort exploring the transitional space. The impact is that essential complex or divergent aspects become hidden from sight. While the unseen aspects do not always challenge initial execution, they tend to crystallise as the change journey unfolds. The unintended outcomes can result in increased disruption and a wide range of operational dysfunctions that can be difficult to quantify as the change process gets underway. Leaders and organisations then find themselves having to cope with the impact of unnecessary complexities and ambiguities that can also inform harder to identify aspects like workforce morale, motivation and commitment.

Impatience Acting into the symptoms of oversimplification and haste, straightforward tasks like clarifying purpose, conducting stakeholder and workforce engagement strategies become deprioritised over execution and delivery. The combined impact is often referred to as 'resistance to change', where the workforces are expected to adopt different operational practices, requiring the acquisition of new knowledge and skills without fully understanding the context for change. The outcome is that leaders become unable to see or grasp the specifics of what the transformation process requires. In practice it is no surprise that they then find the process of transitioning from old to new somewhat of a challenge.

The combined outcomes of oversimplification, haste and impatience create a complex web of interwoven dynamics that can erect a veil on the change agenda. Leaders then find that working with the real complexities of their organisational transformation agendas even more challenging than they need to be in practice.

Transitions: We Don't Know What We Don't Know

There is no doubt that the advancement in technology is facilitating the symptoms of transition blindness. With so much information immediately available at the end of our fingertips, we have become expected to have instant answers and clearly defined solutions to problems. If we want to know something, Google is our best friend, and as a result, there seems to be little patience and tolerance for not-knowing in today's organisations. Unfortunately, Google does not have all the answers when it comes to navigating transitions. The key contributing factor as to why these symptoms appear in organisations is that we do not have enough knowledge and understanding about the complex dynamics of transitions. In particular how transitional processes impact the performance of individuals, teams and organisations.

In my 20-year quest to understand more about the complexities and dynamics of a vast range of organisational transitions, I have formed the view that transitions are complex, ambiguous and messy, what today is now more commonly termed as VUCA (volatility, uncertainty, complexity, ambiguity), a term adopted by the US Army War College in 2002, derived from the theories of Bennis and Nanus (1985).

One of the main challenges of my exploration journey has been the shortage of literature about the multifaceted, complex dynamics of transitions in general. While this book is a practitioner resource, in the spirit of creating context, I find that it helps to at least have some highlights into the different perspectives on transitions. What follows is a high-level summary of my interpretation and discoveries of the literature and different perspectives on transitions.

Three-Stage Frameworks

Schwartz-Salant and Stein (1991) along with other Jungian analysts explore concepts of 'liminality'. It is a term derived from the Latin word 'limen' meaning doorway or threshold. Liminality was first used as a term of discourse in 1909 to describe primitive initiation ceremonies of early adolescence. Folklorist Van Gennep (1960), in his text 'Rites of Passage', proposed three transitional stages:

1. *Separation*
2. *Liminality*
3. *Incorporation*

Liminality as a concept is utilised in Jungian psychology to refer to a threshold between conscious and unconscious portions of the mind. The term 'subliminal' relates to the psychological territory that sits below the threshold of conscious awareness. Stein (1983) has drawn on the concept of liminality to describe the psychological impact of mid-life transitional processes.

I found the concept of liminality fascinating, from a psychological perspective, although not quite so easily transferable, to an organisational change practice, for several reasons. Firstly, even after studying six different psychotherapeutic disciplines, Jungian language took time to decipher and learn. It was not something I could just share and use with business leaders; it required significant translation into straightforward organisational terms. Although not an impossible task, a vital component was missing; I could not fully answer the question of what happens in the liminal space.

Bridges (2004) provided a glimmer of hope by proposing that transitional processes start with an ending and finish with a beginning, a concept that appeared to align with van Gennep's and Jungian psychology's perspectives of liminality. Bridges proposes that there are three phases in a transition process:

Phase 1 Ending, losing, letting go
Phase 2 Neutral zone
Phase 3 New beginning

At first glance, the three-phase concepts of Bridges appeared to be more accessible, in business terms and the context of organisational change. In his text 'Managing Transitions' (2009), Bridges attempts to translate how to deal with the three phases of transition by providing case studies and checklists for organisational managers and leaders. Although in practice, when it came to trying to apply Bridges's suggestions, the task was not straightforward.

The primary challenge was Phase 2 – neutral zone. When the leaders who were experimenting with this concept and I tried to apply the suggested principles to our organisational experiences, the impact felt like the equivalent of stepping into a black hole. Bridges shares some thoughts on the neutral zone and makes suggestions, on what to do, the primary one being that when we are in the neutral zone, it is all about surrendering.

Unfortunately surrendering in practice is not a simple straightforward task, particularly in organisations, because of the inherent complex dynamics that transitions evoke. Leaders of organisations who were at the time and still are today under constant pressure to be and be seen in control demonstrate practical progress and show tangible outcomes from their transformation programmes. As one leader put it:

"Yeah right, surrender to what exactly? It sounds so simple and yet, not quite that straight-forward for when I have to deliver results".

Trying to interpret Bridges's description of the neutral zone left me with felt sense qualities of an in-between space within an in-between space, a principle that within itself was complex and ambiguous. So while Bridges seemed to have shone some light into the dynamics of transitions, the neutral zone still represented an ambiguous unknown context.

Whist these authors acknowledge the challenges associated with liminal space and the neutral zone the key challenge appeared to be the multifaceted complexities of the transitional space. One of the core findings of my transition research over the years is that honouring complexity is a crucial factor while navigating the transitional space. The core principle being that when leaders and organisations try to oversimplify the transitional space, they unintentionally get in their own way.

Another aspect that these authors overlook is 'why' the transitional space is so complex and challenging. My personal experiences have taught me that without knowing the 'why', the causes of transitional challenges, we can struggle to know what to do and how to work with them. The impact is that we can limit our choices in how to approach and work with the complexities of transitions, and revert to known practices only to find that they are not fit for purpose. The combination of oversimplification and not-knowing the 'why' and 'how' creates the potential for unnecessary complexity and ambiguity. Unfortunately, the impact of unnecessary complexity and ambiguity can be like pouring petrol onto a fire of an organisational change agenda, a topic that we will explore in greater depth in Chap. 7.

I have also found a key success factor is how transitional experiences are approached. Using the term managing Bridges takes what I term as a control-focused approach. The impact in practice is that control biased approaches can be perceived as being forceful when we are on the receiving end of them. Over the years, I discovered that when organisations use control-focused approaches and practices to navigate change and implement transitions, they unknowingly introduce fear-based responses. Unfortunately, fear and associated anxiety responses create the potential for overwhelm, paralysis and ultimately, dysfunction in organisations. These are aspects that introduce more challenges to what in some instances can already be complicated tasks. At best, the impact is to stall the transition process; in worst-case scenarios these aspects can completely derail a transformation agenda. The outcomes are unintended consequences that can have significant implications on operational functioning, morale and motivation, factors that we will explore in greater depth in Chap. 5.

Alternative Transition Perspectives

Positioned in the context of an approach for leading change, Scharmer's (2009) Theory U has attempted to address some of the oversimplification challenges by exploring topics related to organisational complexity. Scharmer has also shed light into the 'how' with the seven essential leadership capabilities (holding the space of listening, observing, sensing, presencing, crystallising, prototyping, co-evolving). What appears to be overlooked is depth in the underpinning dimensions of the 'why'. There is also the additional challenge of how Theory U is illustrated, that appears somewhat contradictory and confusing to the reader. Scharmer states that Theory U is not intended to be a linear structured process, although the framework is presented in a left to right form, that in applied terms reflects a linear five-step left to right journey. It is a visual representation that appears to be more in alignment with Kubler-Ross's (1969) five-stage Grief Curve that also became known as the Change Curve in the 1970s and 1980s. Another linear framework, presented in a left to right format that unfortunately, did not fit with the realities of how my colleagues and leaders were practically experiencing change in organisations at the time.

One of the reasons why existing literature has not fully addressed the complexities of the transitional space is that it is tailored for and aimed at the Western mind-set, a simplified, control biased frame-of-reference that has been dominant in the world of organisations for centuries. What these authors have achieved is to provide glimpses into perspectives of transitions that were present and prominent at the time of authorship. My research has revealed that further elaboration and greater depth of insight into the transitional space is a core requirement to support leaders and organisations to succeed with their challenges of today.

Comparing and contrasting the highs and lows of individual, team and organisational transitions, I found that navigating successful transitions is more aligned to the process of transcendence. In Latin terms, the meaning of transcendence is to climb or go beyond something. More akin to the experience of climbing a spiral staircase than a straight linear left to right journey. It is a perspective of transitions that we will elaborate in more detail in Chap. 3.

Impermanence Versus Our Western Mind-Set

The term disruption is currently positioned as something new in our world of business. In practice, what it is actually doing is drawing our awareness to how our world is. Today we are not being given any choice in overlooking or avoiding how we engage with continuous change and transitions, because the evolution of science and technology impacts so many aspects of our lives.

Impermanence or Anicca (Gethin 1998), as it is known in Buddhist psychology, is a state of being that is transitory. It is something that is not permanent, lasting or durable. Just looking within and out into our immediate environment provides some clues. We have a thought, and, moments later, our thought is replaced by another thought. We may wake up feeling happy and contented, step out of bed and trip over the cat and seconds later, we have experienced a shift in our physical and emotional state. Our days circle from daytime through to night. The weather and our seasons are continuous cycles of unpredictable change. From the time we are born, we are growing and developing; when our physical bodies have developed, we transition from growth into ageing. The same principles apply to what we believe to be solid and permanent physical structures. Science has drawn awareness to what appears to be fixed and solid is, at a molecular level, actually continuously changing. It is just that the molecules move at a different rate than our naked eye can see. For example, the ink on paper will fade and, eventually, the paper will disintegrate. Left outside in the elements, the chair that I am sat on while writing this text will tarnish, rust, decay and eventually fall apart.

The key message I took from exploring Complex Adaptive Systems (Kauffman 1995), Chaos Theory (Lewin 1992; Waldrop 1994; Gleick 1988) and Complexity Theory (Gell-Mann 1995; Holland 1995) is that the universe is interconnected, impermanent and in processes of continuous change. As a result, there is inherent complexity that generates processes of deconstruction and reconstruction that in turn create the potential to facilitate change and transformation. From an organisational perspective, Stacey's (2001) concept of Transformative Teleology articulates these processes of continuous transition, although also glided over what happens in the in-between state of the movement from what is known to the unknown. Intellectually, these principles make sense and yet when we come to apply these to our inner world experiences, day-to-day realities and particularly organisational change, accepting and being with impermanence is a different matter. In practice, impermanence is complex and unpredictable. If impermanence is all around us and everything is in a constant state of flux, why is it so difficult to be with what is and go with the flow? Why do we, as individuals, organisations and society, in general, find accepting the reality of impermanence so challenging?

The culprit as Hutchins (2014) proposes is our Western mind-set, a focus on simplicity and control that has evolved over centuries. My belief is that the term change management has erected a veil on our consciousness, the equivalent of a blindfold that impacts how we see and engage with the world, particularly in the context of organisational change. We have become accustomed to creating a false reality that change is something we can manage and control. The impact is that we are not engaging with the way the world is, we are responding to it in the way we want it to be, generating a belief and frame-of-reference that we can control change.

The concept of controlling change has been embedded into how organisations are designed and operate. For example, structured hierarchies, operational processes, enforcing the compliance of rules and regulations, programme and project methodologies, these are all designed to reduce complexity and stop organisations from being out of control. By applying and following clearly defined methodologies, processes, policies and procedures, beliefs and expectations have been created that change can be simplified managed and ultimately controlled.

Working with Transitions

The symptoms of transition blindness (oversimplification, haste and impatience) combined with a lack of insight into the 'why' and 'how' of the transitional space is challenging enough to navigate. When we then combine these dimensions with the dilemma of our Western mind-sets, it is not surprising that leaders and organisations find the process of navigating transitions complex and challenging.

We live in a knowledge-biased world. As Sir Francis Bacon (1625) put it, 'Knowledge is power', it has become the foundation for success in today's society. Depth of knowledge known as 'subject matter expertise' influences all aspects of our lives, we only have to look at the range of degree topics that universities are now offering compared to ten years ago. Particularly over the last ten years, specialist skills have become favoured over generalist skillsets.

Organisations hire, develop and promote people on the depth of their knowledge and expertise. Many organisations pride themselves on the knowledge base of their workforces, promoting their expertise as a core competitive advantage. Not-knowing is generally not considered something that leaders like to promote or shout about. Particularly when it comes to leaders of change, who are expected to know, provide certainty and have all the answers to challenges when things do not go to plan. The combined outcomes of all of these factors is the tendency for organisations to skip and overlook the transitional space altogether. Leaders have a habit of taking huge leaps from ideas, intentions and strategies, straight into implementation expecting miraculous outcomes to be implemented and achieved. The outcome is the disruptive and dysfunctional responses that unfortunately impact the effective functioning of organisations, the wellbeing of workforces and bottom-line results. Not-knowing, ambiguity and complexity are factors that are naturally inherent in all processes of transitions. Core contributory factors that when leaders and organisations accept and embrace, they become able to utilise these challenging dimensions to create competitive advantage. It is the positive potential inherent in all processes of transitions that we will inquire into and explore throughout this book. The message is relatively straightforward in today's environment; organisations have to work with the world the way it is not just the way they want it to be. The core principle is that we can't manage change, our challenge today is learning how to work with it.

Summary
What we have explored in this chapter are the foundations for why we as human beings, leaders and organisations find navigating transitions challenging. How the factors of oversimplification, haste and impatience contribute to the impact of transition blindness, its impact and why it has become a common leadership and organisation ailment. We have reviewed the challenges with the current literature on transitions that inform existing change leadership practices. Plus perspectives that unveil how the concept of change man-

agement is built on primary needs for simplicity and control. All of these aspects inform a Western historical paradigm that unfortunately now is no longer fit for purpose for leading the complexities of change in today's organisations. The rest of this book aims to shed light and deepen understanding into the 'why' and answer the key question at the forefront of most change leaders' minds: 'so what do we do about it?'

An Invitation for Self-Inquiry

One of the key contributing factors I have found that supports leaders to work with transitions is systemic insight. Systemic insight is about being able to understand the multifaceted, interconnected aspects and complexities informing change agendas, preferably at the outset of the change process.

In supporting leaders to develop transition leadership capabilities, I have found that the most helpful way of understanding working with this practice is to start with a personal experience. As we are about to embark on a journey of exploring the transitional space in greater depth, the invitation is to start with inquiring into one of your own transitional experiences. The intent is that exploring your experiences upfront will support applied practical insight throughout the rest of this book. Here are a few questions, to support the start of your inquiry journey:

1. *Transition* – choose something that is currently in transition for you today.
2. *Complexity* – what is known and unknown about your transition?
3. *Experience* – what thoughts, emotions, feelings are present for you now?
4. *Impact* – how are your experiences influencing your behaviour with yourself/others?
5. *Outcomes* – what is the combined result of your experiences and behaviours?

If you have more of your own questions, my encouragement is to explore them. I have found that regardless of the levels of complexity, the more information we have at the beginning of a transitional journey, the more resources we have to work with in practice. It is helpful to record your responses as we will utilise and incrementally build on these at the end of each chapter.

Study Tip 1.1
If you are studying in the field of business psychology or organisational development, then it is worth investing time to understand the different theories and perspectives on transitions. This inquiry process will help you develop your own frame-of-reference for how our world has interpreted the field of transitions to date.

References

Bacon, F. (1625). Essayes or counsels, civill and morall. https://en.wikipedia.org/wiki/Essays_(Francis_Bacon)

Bennis, W., & Nanus, B. (1985). *Leaders: Strategies for taking charge*. New York: Collins.

Bridges, W. (2004). *Transitions. Making sense of Life's changes*. New York: Lifelong Books.

Bridges, W. (2009). *Managing transitions. Making the most of change*. London/Boston: Nicholas Breasley Publishing.

Gell-Mann, M. (1995). *The quark and the jaguar: Adventures in the simple and complex*. London: Abacus.

Gethin, R. (1998). *The foundations of Buddhism*. Oxford: Oxford University Press.

Gleick, J. (1988). *Chaos: Making a new science*. New York: Abacus.

Holland, J. H. (1995). *Hidden order: How adaptation builds complexity*. New York: Helix Books, Addison-Wesley.

Hutchins, G. (2014). *The illusion of separation*. Edinburgh: Floris Books.

Kauffman, S. (1995). *At home in the universe*. New York: Oxford University Press.

Kübler-Ross, E. (1969). *On death and dying*. New York: Routledge.

Lewin, R. (1992). *Complexity: Life at the edge of Chaos*. New York: Macmillan.

Scharmer, C. O. (2009/2016). *Theory U. leading from the future as it emerges. The social technology of presencing*. San Francisco: Berrett-Kehler Publishers.

Schwartz-Salant, N., & Stein, M. (1991). *Liminality and transitional phenomena*. Wilmette: Chiron Publications.

Stacey, R. (2001). *Complex responsive processes in organisations*. London: Routledge.

Stein, M. (1983). *In midlife*. Asheville: Chiron Publications.

Van Gennep, A. (1960). *Rites of passage*. Chicago: University of Chicago Press.

Waldrop, M. (1994). *Complexity: The emerging science at the edge of order and Chaos*. London: Penguin.

Chapter 3
Territories of Transitions

Introduction

This chapter shines light into the dynamics of the transitional space. It presents the transition cycle, a framework for understanding the complexities and unseen aspects that influence transitional journeys for individuals, teams and organisations. The transition cycle has been created through integrating over 20 years of organisational research, with clinical psychology and Buddhist philosophy to provide depth of insight into the multifaceted dynamics of the transitional process. It highlights fundamental principles that honouring and working with complexity that are essential enablers of leading effective transformation processes in today's environment. That when leaders can see and know the complexities of the transitional space, they can develop approaches for working with them, supporting their organisations to do the same. These practices provide a practical approach to overcoming another leadership challenge of understanding the unknown dimensions that transition processes evoke.

A Shift in Perspective

Organisations of today are in constant states of transition, reorganisations, turnrounds and start-ups. Boards are continuously seeking to implement strategies, reengineer processes and carry through improvement and transformation programmes to secure success and competitive market advantage. Teams form and re-form as members; leaders and projects come and go. Projects are assembled to support the launch of new businesses and products, rearranged to improve the provision of services, realigning resources to respond to economic and market conditions.

As employees of organisations, we are assigned, appointed, rotated, promoted and called upon to come to terms with the changes in circumstances and requirements.

© Springer Nature Switzerland AG 2020
C. Hayes, *Transition Leadership*, https://doi.org/10.1007/978-3-030-42787-0_3

We are required to learn new skills and knowledge, to take on different responsibilities, to meet expectations and deliver successful, profitable tangible outcomes.

Developing careers is an evolving journey of multiple processes of transitions over time. Becoming an employee for the first time, we go through a period of formal and informal development. Transitioning into acquiring the competence to work with minimal supervision, we learn to recognise what needs to be done and delivered without having to be directed. As we deepen our sills, knowledge and competencies, we step into new territory of supervising others and encountering the challenges of learning how to manage, motivate and develop teams. Developing the core skills of knowing how to resolve competing demands for resources and attention, we transition into the role of becoming an organisational leader. The final transitional challenge is figuring out how to co-ordinate, integrate and create on a bigger scale, nurturing and developing the next generation, as we hand over and move on.

I am sure some if not all of these examples are familiar experiences of working in and being part of organisations. Having experienced all of these examples in many different contexts, I would not say that any of these transitional experiences was a simple A to B or left to right journey. What I have uncovered over the years is that effectively working with the transitional space requires a shift in how we see the concept of change and how we engage with our experiences of it.

Tibetan Bardos

While researching the concept of impermanence and the impact of Western mindsets in organisations, I came across the teachings of Tibetan Bardos. Comparing my organisational change and transformation experiences, with the philosophical context of the Bardos, I found many synergies. It was as though a light had been shone into a tunnel of darkness, illuminating the unknown and unseen dimension of why navigating change in organisations were such challenging experiences in multiple contexts.

The Bardo teachings are ancient Tibetan texts from the Dzogchen Tantras. The term Bardo 'Bar' meaning 'in-between' and 'do' meaning 'suspended' was brought into Western light by the American scholar W. Y. Evans-Wentz in the 'Tibetan Book of the Dead', also known as the 'Bardo Todrol Chenmo' Rinpoche (2002).

The Dzogchen Tantras have been interpreted in a number of different forms over the evolution of different Buddhist philosophies. It took two years to decipher the assumed knowledge from how the different Buddhist traditions had interpreted the Dzogchen practice, mainly as they were initially intended to accompany oral transmission from Tibetan masters. There was also the bonus of the controversy over Evans-Wentz's translation itself. The general view being that he was not a Dzogchen practitioner and the fact that there was a significant timeframe between when the texts were originally written to when they were translated.

After comparing and contrasting between the different perspectives, I settled on the interpretation that the Bardos represented stages of transition, evolution and transcendence. Aspects of lived experience that are situated in the context of the past that has occurred, and a future, that is yet to be manifested. In the traditional philosophical sense, the Bardo texts are the intermediate states between death and rebirth. What follows is a summary of my interpretation of the Bardos and how they translate into an organisational context.

According to various authors, Trungpa and Freemantle (1975), Rangdrol (1987) Rinpoche (2002) and Lodu (2010), there are four types of Bardo experiences:

1. *Natural Bardo of this life*
2. *Painful Bardo of dying*
3. *Luminous Bardo of dharmata*
4. *Karmic Bardo of becoming*

Natural Bardo of This Life   This spans the whole of our lifetime and refers to the space between the time of birth and death. It covers the experience of our waking reality, positive and negative actions, and how we interpret our world through our conditioned habitual tendencies. In short, what we see is what we look for, and what we look for is what we see.

The term often used to describe this in organisations is business as usual (BAU), the different facets of experience that we consider to be the way things are. BAU ranges from known practices, processes, policies and procedures that individuals and teams follow to how people relate to one another and how they approach their day-to-day activities. As one leader put it, *"This is how we do things around here"*. BAU also relates to known thinking patterns, world perspectives and ultimately, what are considered to be cultural norms for how organisations operate and business is conducted.

Painful Bardo of Dying   This is the process of reaching the end of our natural lifespan and generally consists of two phases of dissolution: the outer dissolution, of our physical body, when the senses and elements dissolve, and an inner dissolution of the subtler thought and emotional states of mind. It is known as painful because we are reminded of the complex dynamics of impermanence.

In an organisational context, this relates to interrupting known aspects of what is considered to be the norm. Norms relate to processes, practices, systems, including patterns in thinking and behaviour. It is the beginning of a process of stepping from something that is known into what is unknown. This is the point where leaders and their workforces begin to experience aspects of the uncertainty of an unknown future, while still being aware of what was known in the past.

Luminous Bardo of Dharmata   According to Rinpoche (2002) the Sanskrit word 'dharmata' means the essence of things as they are. It marks the end of the dissolution process and an opening of a new dimension. This is a process of unfolding of mind from its purest state. What is known as the potential for everything, like a clear sky at dawn just before sunrise. The context of this Bardo is experiencing what is, as it is, with unobstructed senses, perception and wisdom.

For organisations, this is where BAU and norms no longer exist as was. Known operating practices have disintegrated and dissolved, waiting to be replaced by something new and different. Leaders and their workforces become challenged with letting go of their world-views, familiar or habitual ways of working, patterns in thinking and behaviour, while the new and different are reforming. This is the threshold where organisations experience complexity uncertainty and ambiguity in many different shapes and forms, faced with the reality of an unknown ambiguous present and a future that has not fully formed.

Karmic Bardo of Becoming Known as 'Sipa' (Lodu 2010) in Tibetan, translated as becoming, possibility or existence. The general view is that if liberation is not achieved in any of the previous Bardo states, our habitual tendencies become reawakened. It is known as 'Karmic Bardo of Becoming' because it is an automatic result of our previous actions. No conscious choice or decisions have been made in the form of the direction we take. The direction of what is being reborn will depend on the karmic notion of what has previously existed.

The karmic Bardo of becoming puts the whole concept of Bardos and transformation into perspective. We have many opportunities to transform, including our capacity to allow different aspects to die, and new facets to be reborn. In the process of rebirth, there is the potential to transcend into something completely new or reform what has been before. If we can develop an acceptance of endings/loss and be with what is we have choice over what becomes. The more we ignore, grasp and refrain from letting go in fear of death and endings, the higher the chance of repeating the old and being stuck in patterns of historical reality. We can move with what is and accept what is becoming, or we painstakingly strive to keep things as they are, despite the fact that things are continually changing. In short we can create new aspects or reincarnate aspects of the old.

These concepts relate to individuals, teams and whole organisations; this is the phase in the transitional space where the opportunity for transformation can take place. It requires the ability to embrace and work with not-knowing and ambiguity. We become faced with the reality of replicating more of the same of what is known or transforming into something different. In practice, this is the acid test to see if plans and aspirations can be transformed into tangible outcomes. Alternatively, if there is attachments to known ways of operating this can prevent new strategies, practices, approaches from being created, realised and put into practice. The outcome is being able to use ambiguity as a springboard for innovation for creating new potential. It is the difference that creates the difference for successful and profitable organisations today.

Bardo Summary

Bringing these philosophical concepts into a resourceful perspective of transitions, movement through the natural Bardo of this life is to accept what is. The opportunity in the painful Bardo of dying is to allow something to disintegrate, dissolving aspects that create blocks to the pathway of liberation. The luminous Bardo of dharmata creates the potential to recognise what is, let things follow their course and untangle interlinked clouded, self-generating perceptions. In the karmic Bardo of becoming, the potential exists to transform into new and different or reinforce known aspects of lived experiences.

The Impact of Transitions

Reflecting on my own life transitions and experiences in organisations, I began to see that the Bardos provided insights into what Diltz (1990) describes as 'Logical levels' of experience (environment, behaviours, skills, knowledge, values/beliefs, identity and spiritual). The core principle is that in navigating our day-to-day lived experiences in organisations, we can often be trying to process multiple transitions simultaneously. A concept that illuminated and explained why leaders reported feeling overwhelmed with their change experiences. Many leaders found that their roles required them to hold a range of different types of transitions within themselves, for their teams and the broader organisational context, at different logical levels of experience simultaneously. The Bardos provided a comprehensive framework, for making the implicit explicit, by drawing awareness to the complexities of multiple types of transitions experienced in organisational environments on a daily basis.

Stages of Evolution and Transcendence

Delving deeper into trying to join up the dots across the different Buddhist doctrines and author perspectives, the word that kept repeating itself in many different contexts was transcendence. Transcendence is something that is beyond our normal physical experience, what I have come to see as an evolving process of unfolding. Like a tulip, when the flower dies, the head and stem eventually disintegrate and dissolve, while the bulb is storing nutrients during the winter. The whole plant enters into a process of transition, forming a new stem so that the flower can bloom in the spring. As I sensed the meaning of transcendence, images of spiral staircases came to mind. While we are in the process of climbing a spiral staircase, it can be challenging to see the pathway that is emerging above us. As we take each step that appears before us, we find ourselves on a journey of stepping from something known into an unknown context, not knowing what the pathway ahead may hold.

Building on the notion of the spiral staircase, I began to see the Bardos as an integrated cycle, comprised of four distinct phases of potential evolution (Fig. 3.1).

Phase 1 *Shifting* – dimension/s of inner/outer experience begin to shift
Phase 2 *Ending* – aspects of familiar inner/outer experiences end
Phase 3 *Emerging* – new/different aspects begin to emerge
Phase 4 *Forming* – new dimensions and facets begin to come into form

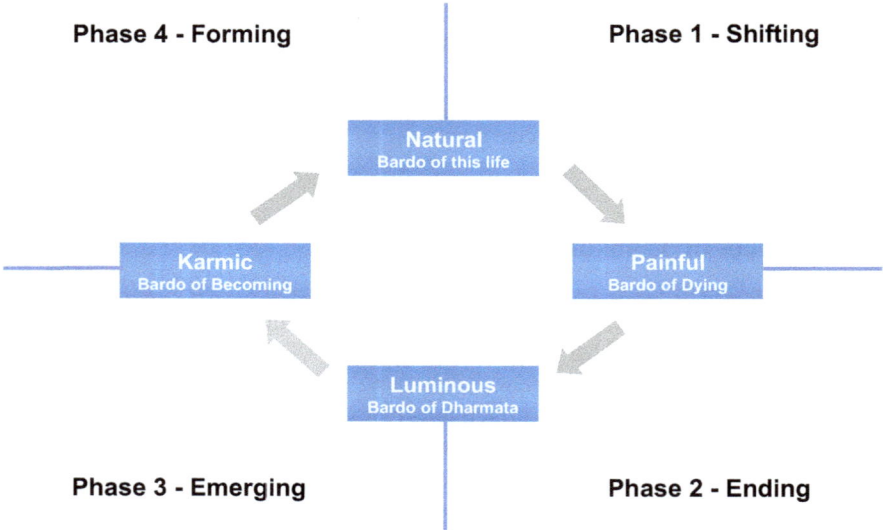

Fig. 3.1 Bardo cycle and phases of evolution

I have come to view the transitional journey as a flow of movement through the Bardo phases where transformation into new/different takes place when the full cycle has been completed. I have chosen to present this model in an east to west format because the learning from my organisational change practice is that transformation requires stepping out of old ground to transcend into new. The notion that true transformation cannot fully take place until we evolve through all four phases.

Transition Processes and Gateways

Piloting and testing this framework in my clinical and organisational practice for two years, I began to notice there were repeating patterns that appeared in a wide range of different transition experiences. These patterns represented distinct evolving processes that accompanied and facilitated movement through the different Bardo phases. Evolving processes that as one change leader put it, *"the in-between states that facilitated movement from one Bardo phase to the next"* (Fig. 3.2).

Phase 1 *Shifting* – dismantling and deconstructing the norm
Phase 2 *Ending* – disintegrating and dissolving the known
Phase 3 *Emerging* – reforming and reconstructing potential
Phase 4 *Forming* – developing and transcending into new form

Reflecting on my own and organisation experiences, I do not believe it is possible to skip phases; I am also of the view that there is no consistency or defined timeline. Each transitional experience is subject to different situational

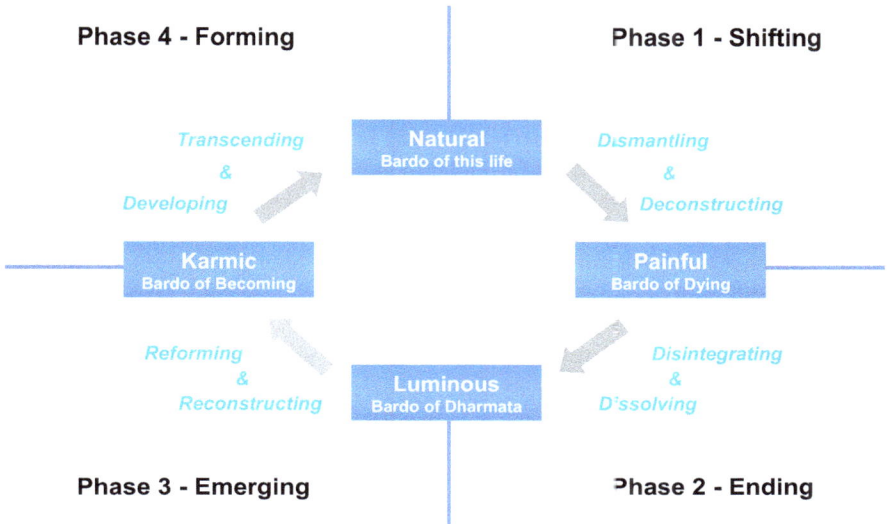

Fig. 3.2 Transition processes and gateways

circumstances and the associated complexities of the responses that they evoke. I have experienced some leaders move through the whole cycle in one coaching session and yet while trying to navigate a different type of transitional process, struggle and get stuck in one particular phase. For example, it can often be easier to dismantle, deconstruct and change our perspective on a relationship with a work colleague, than a close friend or family member and vice versa depending on the nature of the relationship.

Combining the Bardo phases with the accompanying evolving processes transformed my perspective on the whole cycle. I began to see and experience that in practice, what the Bardos represented were gateways. That the reason why individuals, teams and organisations were struggling to navigate transitional processes was that they had not fully crossed a particular gateway. Despite what appeared on the surface to be lots of activities and effort, in practice, the outcomes reflected that they were somehow held in different transitional phases. As with a garden gate, they had to fully step over a threshold to move into a different phase. I began to see that each gateway had a particular purpose that represented distinct qualities of activities.

Natural Bardo of the life = Consolidating norms
Painful Bardo of dying = Interrupting patterns
Luminous Bardo of dharmata = Letting go
Karmic Bardo of becoming = Creating new

These insights revealed that some of the challenges that individuals, teams and organisations were having with transitions seemed to be associated with not fully embracing the associated activities of each gateway. What got in the way of this was facing and often revisiting the complex facets of interconnected patterns of the known and unknown aspects that were informed by or linked to a particular phase. For example, it can be incredibly challenging to interrupt patterns in behaviours if people are trying to cope with dismantling and deconstructing what they have come to know as the norm. In the process of disintegrating and dissolving, world views and perspectives being able to let go of what is known can be challenging if the alternative paradigm has not yet been clearly defined. While reforming and reconstructing new working practices, investing time and resources to start with a blank piece of paper can often be experienced as overwhelming and step too far.

In all phases, staying with what is known despite how challenging or dysfunctional it maybe can often take centre stage. What influences these responses is projected fear of the unknown and attachment to what is known, driven by an inherent need to want to gain certainty, and achieve stability in trying to control outcomes. The unintentional impact can be to derail aspects of the transitional journey, creating a magnetic pull to maintain sameness in what is known that can be present at any phase of the Bardo cycle. In practice this presents a whole range of challenging experiences that we will explore in more detail in Chap. 4.

In all phases of transition, we are continuously navigating a gravitational pull between past, present and future experiences. Building on a neuroscientific perspective, it is like the functioning of the way our human brains work. We reference memories from the past, bringing them into the present and project them into the future. In practical terms navigating transitional processes means, we have to pass the test of working with the magnetic pull of the known and familiar from the past in order to move forward into new territories.

Over the years, I have lost count of the number of factors that I have tried to kid myself that I have transformed. Only to find that elements and aspects that I believed I had transformed return presented in a different context like the same fruit in a different bowl. Leaders find that while working with these push-pull challenges, a lot of insights can be gained from drawing awareness to the complexities of déjà vu experiences. Drawing awareness to past and present tensions can be key to unlocking fixed frames-of-reference, dysfunctional behaviours and operational practices in many different organisational contexts. I find that it is incredibly resourceful to inquire into the causes of push/pull tensions. The insights gained from processes of inquiry can provide informed choice in how to respond and proceed with the interwoven complexities of transitional experiences.

Honouring Complexity

Applying and utilising the Bardo concepts in organisations reveals why Google cannot provide us with all the answers to navigating the transitional space. The primary reason being that these concepts highlight the multifaceted dynamics and dimensions of the different levels of complexity that we are required to navigate when it comes to leading change. In practice, this means that honouring and engaging with complexity are core capabilities for working with the transitional space. There is no one right or wrong answer, just because something is complex does not mean it is impossible. In practice, transitions take investment in time and resources to work through the challenges that they initiate. One of my most significant insights into successful transformations is that when organisations honour the complexities of their change agendas, they can work with them. I have found that organisations that intentionally incorporate honouring and working with complexity into their day-to-day operational functioning, fully utilise the outcomes to create a competitive market advantage.

This principle relates to both the 'what and how' of people, process and technical aspects. By adopting a narrowly focused perspective on their agendas, change leaders can become susceptible to the activities that take place outside of their frames-of-reference. For example, while the focus of implementing new software is technology biased, it will also involve and impact people, processes, risk, regulatory and compliance requirements. If the interdependent aspects are overlooked, then the implementation and transformation processes can be at risk. By investing in exploring complexities at the beginning and during the execution of a transitional journey, leaders can successfully navigate the challenges of transformation. Honouring complexity facilitates a more resourceful approach, significantly reducing the risks of becoming side-lined or overwhelmed by unseen dimensions that emerge on the pathway towards implementation.

The key message I am highlighting is that there are more dimensions of complexity to our lived experiences of transitions than can be immediately apparent at the outset of a change process. That when we do not consider complex factors while trying to navigate the transitional space, we run the risks of becoming challenged, stuck and overwhelmed by our experiences. When leaders actively seek to understand and work with the complexities of the systemic functioning of their organisations, they become resourceful. In practice, it means that they can leverage diversity of thought to gain new/different perspectives and alternative ways of approaching and working with their transformation challenges. When leaders invest time in understanding and working with the complexities of the transitional space, they can mitigate the risks that oversimplification, haste and impatience create.

The Transition Cycle

Feedback from change leaders was that seeing the gateways and the associated phases illuminated the transitional space. To utilise the concepts as a frame-of-reference to support as one leader put it, *"to understand and connect with the experiences of what operating in a VUCA environment means in practice"*. As a conceptual resource for providing a comprehensive way of seeing, making sense of the inherent complex dynamics that often go unnoticed in organisations. A resourceful framework that offered a new perspective and lens to see nuances and dimensions and bring light into the darker, complex, ambiguous aspects that the journey of navigating transitions evokes.

Phase 4 - Forming   **Phase 1 - Shifting**

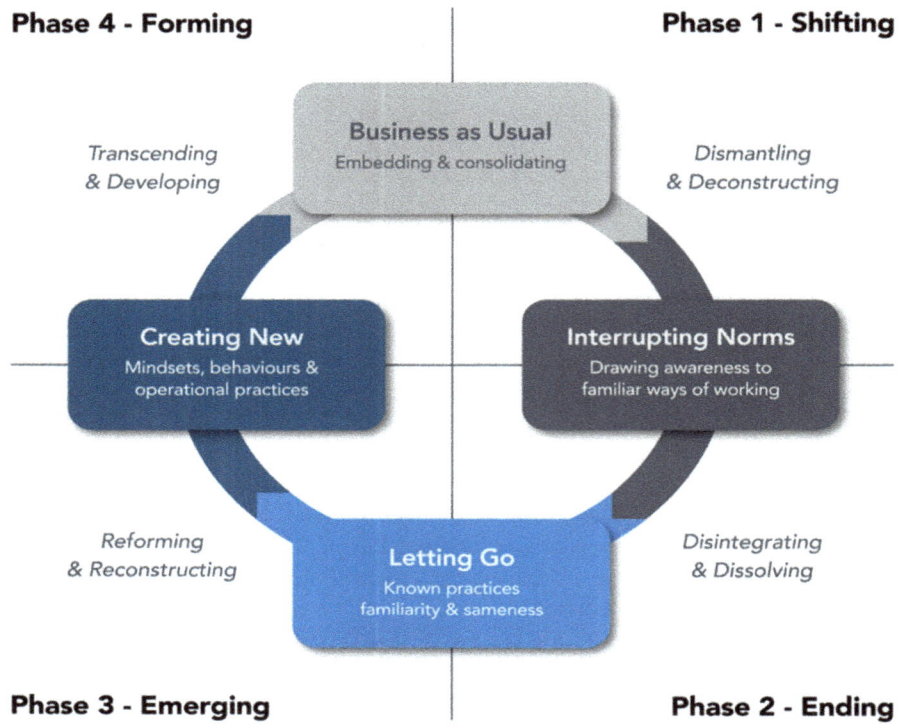

Transcending   *Dismantling*
& Developing   *& Deconstructing*

Reforming   *Disintegrating*
& Reconstructing   *& Dissolving*

Phase 3 - Emerging   **Phase 2 - Ending**

Fig. 3.3 Transition cycle

The third evolution of the transition framework was to make the principles more accessible to a broader audience, that required translating the Bardos into organisational terms, what has now become known as the transition cycle (Fig. 3.3).

Utilising the Transition Cycle in Organisations

The core purpose of the transition cycle is to shed light into the unknowns of the transitional space. Since its development in 2008, it has become a resource for supporting individuals, teams and organisations to gain insight into a wide range of different transitional experiences.

Planning Utilised as a map for designing and planning change projects and transformation programmes at the outset. To provide insight into the different dimensions of territories that may be required to be navigated and to gain a perspective on the nature of transitional territories and pathways ahead.

Monitoring A through-time orientation resource for supporting inquiry and insight, as the dynamics of the transformation journey unfolds. Just like the process of reviewing a road map, when we have begun the journey, it can be helpful to gain a perspective of where we are and a sense of the route that lies ahead.

Insight To uncover, make sense and understand the unknown foundations and origins of complex challenges. To illuminate how people may be unintentionally getting in their own way by not-knowing the multifaceted dimensions that transitions evoke.

Case studies 3.1, 3.2 and 3.3 illustrate applied examples of how individuals, teams and organisations have utilised the transition cycle. We will explore the application and more examples of the use of the transition cycle throughout in the following chapters.

Case Study 3.1 Individual: James's Shift in Perspective

After 25 years of developing a successful career as a technology specialist, James had been promoted to be the Senior Executive of a new division. Four months into the role, James was finding his new position extremely challenging. The new management team that he had created were not collaborating with each other. He was also getting feedback from his immediate boss that a number of his direct reports were complaining about his behaviour, communication and leadership styles. The view was that James was disempowering his direct reports and not returning authority to his leadership team for the functioning of the division. James knew somehow that he needed to make changes he just was not clear what to do or where to start.

As we explored the different dynamics of his challenge and the principles of the transition cycle, James could see the root cause of his challenges. Following a specialist career path for the whole of his career, James had focused his attention on developing depth in technical knowledge. James had directed his attention on applying his specialist knowledge in his day-to-day activities. These were key attributes that historically, James had been sponsored and rewarded for that had also contributed to his promotion into his new Executive role.

James recognised that he needed to shift his perspectives and patterns of behaviours in many different contexts. For example, dismantling and deconstructing, his known and preferred ways of working, like interrupting and catching himself from diving into the technical detail at divisional leadership meetings. Letting go of his primary need to know all the answers, inviting and encouraging his team to contribute and provide input into solving complex problems. It also meant creating a new focused leadership purpose to build an effective leadership team, and focus his attention on understanding and supporting development of the new division.

Exploring the transition cycle supported James to see what was causing his immediate challenges. Plus where he could shift his perspective, the new practices that he had to learn to develop and where he had to focus his attention on his role going forward.

Case Study 3.2 Team: Ending Known Project Practices

A regulatory project team had been active for 12 months, and they were struggling to achieve critical deliverables. During that period, they saw the come and go of two programme leads and two project managers. People were working 14–15 hour days and time was getting short, as they had six months to deliver a non-negotiable deadline to the regulator. Not meeting the deadline would mean shutting down part of their global business. While sharing their collective experiences, through exploring the transition cycle, the team uncovered that they were caught in a recursive, self-sustaining loop. The project as a whole was circling between the phases of shifting and ending. The reason that they were not achieving their espoused deliverables was that they needed to let some key factors go.

While reviewing and inquiring into the repeating patterns in their behaviours and practices that were sustaining their recursive loop, they uncovered their core challenge. The project team was comprised of regulatory experts. Responding to their fear of not being able to find a pathway through the complex regulatory requirements, they had sourced the project with their most skilled technicians. The collective impact was that every time an expert found a problem, the whole project would come to a halt until they had found a solution and fixed it. The outcomes from the problem-solving exercises resulted in creating alternative pathways that kept changing the approaches and direction of travel for the project as a whole.

What they had not seen was that they needed a diverse range of knowledge and skills to navigate the multifaceted levels of complexity to deliver tangible outcomes. What they lacked were programme and project management capabilities, to contain the complex problem-solving activities and keep the overall project agenda on track. This was an insight that illuminated why people with these skills had either chosen or been invited to leave the project because they had a different strategic focus. The regulatory experts realised that they had not valued the contribution of these roles because they were speaking a different language. When questions were asked like *"why are we getting the drains up on everything again?"* Instead of listening and engaging with the questions of a different frame-of-reference, the regulatory experts dismissed the project managers for not having enough subject matter knowledge about the problem.

Recognising how they were unintentionally getting in their own way, they redeployed their existing regulatory expert who had taken on the responsibilities for leading the project into another role. Within two weeks, they hired a new programme manager and created two new project management roles to incorporate new/different skill sets and capabilities. Despite their challenges, the team managed to comply with the regulatory requirements and deliver their project on time. The transition cycle created the opportunity to inquire and explore the unknown patterns in their thinking and behaviour. It supported the team to see what they could not see at the time and the practical courses of action that would facilitate a productive, successful outcome for the team and the organisation.

Case Study 3.3 Organisation: Creating New Operational Functioning
A large global organisation had embarked on a new restructuring programme. The aspiration was to consolidate all of the finance functions that resided in separate business into one unified division. The purpose was to provide a more integrated support service to their clients and the organisation as a whole. Equipped with a strategy provided by one of the large management consulting firms, six months into their programme, they found themselves challenged to gain any traction. The strategic intent was to introduce a new matrix-based organisational structure; the practical reality was something different. The primary outcomes from their efforts were the formation of specialist horizontal silos. The senior leaders recognised that despite their efforts, all they had done was swapped apples for apples. In practice they had not consolidated anything, what they had achieved was to reform into new separate specialist parts that were operating as intendant units disconnected from each other. Exploring the operational functioning and cultural dynamics of the new division, they discovered many factors had been overlooked. In their haste to implement a new organisational structure, they had not fully explored the multifaceted levels of complexity required to support the transformation at the outset.

As the Executive leaders reflected on their efforts and reviewed them against the transition cycle, they realised that their focus had been directed towards the more tangible aspects. The leaders realised that the new division had transitioned through all four phases in some areas by creating a new structure, functional reporting lines, integrating technology platforms and moving to new physical locations. Their underlying perspective at the outset was that these tangible aspects would create the new division. In practice, the leaders had focused on what they could see, overlooking that they also needed to create and develop new/different frameworks and integrated behaviours to support effective day-to-day functioning. In addition to new technology systems, they also needed new processes for sharing information and collaborating to support a fully functional matrix-based operating mode. The integrated principle also applied to the leadership team. This in practice meant replacing operating as a group of individual contributors, with separate agendas, to developing new ways of working with each other as a fully integrated team. The transition cycle supported the leaders to see and know what they did not know. To clearly define where they could productively focus their attention to move forward and create their desired outcome of a new unified, integrated financial division.

Exploring Edges

Utilising the transition cycle to support leaders and their teams to work with the complexities of their change agendas, collectively we made another discovery. We uncovered patterns in positive and challenging aspects of transitional experiences. Some leaders found that, just entering into Phase 1 held the potential for intrigue and excitement. While for other leaders, the fear of the unknown implications of what might have to be dismantled or deconstructed at the outset of a change journey ranged from challenging to completely overwhelming.

I use the term edges because I have found that patterns in what we like and dislike can be equally challenging. The primary reason is that we are more likely to be drawn towards what we like avoid and overlook what we do not like. Our responses and reactions to edges facilitate where we focus our attention and efforts also have the potential of creating tunnel vision. Just because we do not like something does not mean it is not important. Equally, if we do like something, then questioning what purpose is it serving stops us from following a path out of habit.

As leaders reviewed their different responses and experiences with transitions, they discovered that their reactions were context-driven, depending on the subject that was in transition. For others, they found that regardless of the context, there were some phases and gateways that consistently evoked the same perceptions, feelings, responses and reactions. For example, I was reminded that my repeating patterns appear in Phase 3, served up in the form of impatience, particularly at the earlier stages of my career. I love change, particularly the opportunity to create new and different. Yet, at the time, I often found myself to be standing alone with my enthusiasm, where I was focusing on achieving outcomes, and my colleagues were taking a while to come to terms with emerging phases of reforming and reconstructing a new world.

Despite our positive intentions, unfortunately, it is not always possible to completely erase our edges with the transitional space. Our edges are created by many factors including motivations, needs and life experiences that can often reside in the depths of our unconscious. The key factor is spotting edges when they arrive and where they may make an appearance along the journey. As with my own experience, leaders found that by drawing awareness to their edges, and patterns in responses, they supported and developed their depth of self-insight and understanding. Armed with self-insight leaders found they had choice in how they responded to both themselves and others. Many found it particularly helpful to come to know patterns in the nature of the relationships they had with complexity and ambiguity a practice that we will explore in more depth in the next chapter.

Orientation

Orientation is a key resource for supporting successful transition processes. It is challenging to work with and honour complexity if we are grappling with disorientation. Reactions and responses to disorientation are core factors that can add additional complexities to the transitional space making the journey even more challenging. It is highly likely that there will be many unknowns, we will be short of facts and not have answers to all of our questions. Regardless of what phase or gateway, we are transitioning through it is inevitable that we will find ourselves grappling with edges in some shape or form. That said, having a sense of where we are, where we have been, and the pathway ahead provides a sense of perspective, creating an opportunity for inquiry and reflection. The outcomes from inquiry and reflection create resources to work with the complexities of our current experiences whilst mitigating the risks of making our transitional journeys even more challenging.

Summary
What we have been exploring in this chapter are the dimensions and different territories of transitions, how the transition cycle illuminates the dynamics of complex, multifaceted unseen factors that inform and influence the transitional space. Highlighting why honouring and working with complexity are key enablers of leading effective transformation processes for individuals, teams and organisations in today's environment. Plus how the transition cycle can be utilised to facilitate orientation. A practical resource for designing and planning transformation programmes at the outset, monitoring progress and providing insights to uncover, the unknown foundations and origins of complex transitional challenges.

An Invitation for Self-Inquiry
To bring these concepts and principles to life, the invitation is to apply the transition cycle to your current transitional experience that you chose in Chap. 2. Here are a few questions to support your inquiry:

1. *Phase* – what phase/s does your transition reside within?
2. *Gateway* – what gateway most closely relates to your transition experience?
3. *Present* – what insights do you have about your current experience?
4. *Past* – are there any insight/s from previous experiences, phases or gateways?
5. *Edges* – are there any positive/challenging aspects, present or future?
6. *Impact* – how has knowing the transition cycle impacted your transition experience?
7. *Future* – what does the transitional journey ahead now look like for you?
8. *Outcome* – what impact has exploring the transition cycle had?

As with the previous reflective exercise, if you have more questions, my encouragement is to explore them. Inquiring into where we are, where we have been and where we are going is a resourceful practice for all types of

(continued)

(continued)

transitional journey. The more questions we ask the more options and potential we can generate for ourselves others and organisations. As mentioned above, also expect to have many unknowns, it's all part of the journey. The key factor to keep in mind is that the difference that makes the difference is that it is not the unknowns; it all comes down to the nature of the relationship we have with them. Please record your responses as we will explore the impact of the nature of the relationships we have with the unknown in the next chapter.

References

Dilts, R. (1990). *Changing belief systems with NLP*. California: Meta Publications.
Lodu, L. (2010). *Bardo teachings. The way of death and rebirth*. New York: Snow Lion Publications.
Rangdrol, T. N. (1987). *The mirror of mindfulness*. Hong Kong: Rangjng Yeshe Publications.
Rinpoche, S. (2002). *The Tibetan book of living and dying*. London: Rider.
Trungpa, C., & Freemantle, F. (1975). *The Tibetan book of the dead*. Boston: Shambhala Publications.

Chapter 4
The Impact of Transitions

Introduction

This chapter explores approaches for recognising, understanding and working with ambiguity, which is an inherent natural aspect of all transitional processes. Drawing on clinical psychology, neuroscience and Buddhist philosophy informed by applied research, it unveils the origins, symptoms and impact of ambiguity anxiety; aspects that reveal how the constructs of the Western mind-set contribute to anxiety and fear-based responses. Behavioural responses that unintentionally make the process of navigating change challenging and stressful experiences. It uncovers the foundations for what has generally become termed as 'resistance to change and politics' in organisations. Case studies provide practical insights for learning how to recognise the symptoms of ambiguity anxiety in individuals, teams and organisational environments. It also introduces the concept of the importance of *'knowing the nature of the self-self relationship'* as a core transition leadership competency.

Ambiguity Anxiety

I began investigating the impact of ambiguity in organisations in 2000, during a trend for outsourcing and offshoring that was gaining momentum in the financial services industry. I repeatedly observed leaders with successful track records failing to achieve outcomes. Skilled and intelligent leaders who began to stall their careers, while perfecting the art of political dance, without any known logical reasons. Watching them replace key characteristics that had been at the heart of their successful careers with attributes that derailed their leadership effectiveness. Behaviours that unveiled at the time, what appeared to be the dark side of their personalities.

© Springer Nature Switzerland AG 2020
C. Hayes, *Transition Leadership*, https://doi.org/10.1007/978-3-030-42787-0_4

Aligning my discoveries with Horney (1950) and Hogan and Hogan's (2001) research on derailment factors illuminated that what leaders were acting out was stress and anxiety-related responses (Fig. 4.1).

The psychoanalyst Horney (1950) proposes that under the influence of challenging and anxiety-provoking situations, people adopt these strategies to mitigate risk and achieve psychological and/or physical safety. It is a proposition that correlates with Levine's (1997) concept of fight, freeze and flight responses. The neuroscientific perspective of Hanson (2009) and Siegel (2010) is that due to the way we have evolved as human beings, our physical and mental systems are continuously orientating around reducing threat. In attempt to keep ourselves safe we deploy strategies for trying to create stability, by moving towards opportunities and avoid danger.

Hanson (2009) suggests that when the interrelated systems of our body, mind and relationships with others become unstable, our brains produce uncomfortable signals of threat. Our nervous systems trigger increased levels of cortisol, the primary stress hormone that signals to our bodies and brain that we are in danger, what in neuroscience terms is known as our autonomic nervous stress response system. Connecting this perspective with the Buddhist philosophical concept of impermanence that we explored in Chaps. 2 and 3, as the universe is continuously changing, the potential exists for these threat signals to keep coming. The view of these different authors is that there are distinct purposes behind these strategies.

Move Towards To build protection to minimise the threat of judgement and criticism from others. The presence of this strategy can be seen in behaviours such as perfectionism, micromanaging tasks and people, with the focused intent to reduce

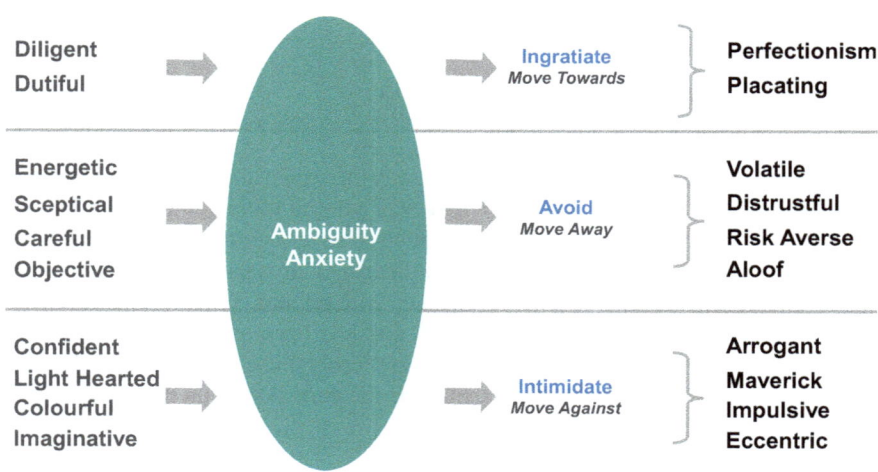

Fig. 4.1 Organisation and transformation derailing factors

risks. It can also show up as placating authority and reluctance to take or hold a position of power for fear of being rejected by others.

Move Against To control, dominate and intimidate others. The presence of this strategy is reflected in behaviours such as arrogance, a need to be seen to know and have all the answers, 'I am right, and you are wrong', 'It is my way or the high way'. Move against strategies can also be presented as impulsiveness, being seen as unpredictable, distracted and unfocused. Alternatively, these strategies can show up as eccentricity, lots of off the wall ideas, supported by undefined and ungrounded perspectives. People who frequently demonstrate these strategies are often referred to as mavericks, who 'fly by the seat of their pants', that are perceived to be challenging to engage and connect with by others.

Move Away To avoid others. This strategy can show up as aloofness, where people keep themselves to themselves, rarely sharing their feelings or emotions. Individuals who frequently deploy these strategies can be labelled as risk-averse or procrastinators that are fearful of making the wrong decisions. Move away strategies can also take the form of criticising and being distrustful of others, with a tendency to focus on the downside. Or alternatively behaviours can take the form of volatility, short-tempered and unpredictable mood swings.

For some leaders, these behaviours seemed to appear out of thin air connected to particular scenarios or events. In others, their stress responses became ingrained in their day-to-day operational behaviours and leadership practices. The outcomes resulted in repeating patterns in behaviours that impacted how their personalities were perceived and the nature of the relationships that they held with others. The suggested reason for the dynamic shifts in behaviour was that the individuals were experiencing some form of midlife crisis. Although, given the volume of what appeared to be extreme examples, I was not convinced. The question at the forefront of my mind was surely not everyone who had started to change their behaviours were having a midlife crisis.

Attempting to understand the drivers for what in some instances appeared as night and day polarised shifts in behaviour, I uncovered that the causes were driven by conscious and unconscious responses to ambiguity. Repeatedly cited reasons for dramatic shifts in behaviours from a wide range of experienced leaders were:

Fear – of failure and the unknown
Attachment – to what was known
Control – requirements to want to manage and guarantee successful outcomes
Entitlement – as leaders they should know

Factors aligned to what Richo (2006) terms as responses to fear, attachment, control and entitlement. The projected fear of what might happen in the future and attachment to what was familiar and known. Requirements to control and have the world the way they wanted it to be and perceived entitlement that leading others required knowing and having all the answers.

The underlying themes in all these responses were that impermanence, not-knowing and ambiguity were perceived as bad that threatened their roles, responsibilities and competence as leaders. Some leaders were aware that in attempting to remove ambiguity, they were adopting different behaviours in the hope of achieving results. For others, they reported feeling stressed, unaware of how they were unknowingly derailing their leadership effectiveness, relationships with others and ultimately, their organisational change agendas.

In organisational environments of continuous change, the conscious and unconscious focus of these leaders was to remove ambiguity from their daily experiences to make their associated challenges go away. Leaders struggled to honour and lead others through the complexities of their change agendas because they were overwhelmed by their responses to not-knowing and ambiguity. Over the years, I have discovered that stress response behaviours are not just acted out by individuals; they also inform practices of teams and organisational cultures.

Case studies 4.1, 4.2 and 4.3 illustrate examples of how individuals, teams and organisations deploy the move towards, against and away from strategies.

Case Study 4.1 Organisation: Moving Towards Safety in Silos

A large healthcare Trust was trying to understand the cause of the increasing numbers of patient complaints. The primary challenge seemed to be the difference in the level of services that they were experiencing between the main hospital and Community Service Centres. Patients reported that the Community Service Centres were supportive and accommodating, and yet when they visited the main hospital, they had a very different experience. The underlying challenge was the misalignment with the services that the patients expected versus what they received in practice. Patient records were out of date, resulting in reports of contradictory diagnosis of conditions, mismatches of medication and delays of treatment.

As we explored the functioning of Community Services and the hospital, we discovered a misalignment of relationships, processes, policies and procedures between both parties.

Being owned and funded by the main hospital, the Community Service Centres perceived that they were not invited to participate in the overall strategic agenda. They reported not being fully represented or engaged in strategic decision-making processes. The outcome was that they felt disempowered with no authority to question or challenge the decisions that they were continuously on the receiving end of, particularly in situations that involved resourcing and cost reduction. The Community Service Centres found themselves caught between a rock and a hard place. The Community Service Centres did not want to upset their patients because they were fearful of the impact of complaint rates. At the same time, they were also fearful of the impact of the potential consequences of challenging Trust's Senior Executives. The outcome was that they said yes to both parties while focusing their attention on attachment to their own Community Services agenda. An agenda that they felt they could control, and the primary strategy for keeping themselves safe. It was not until the patients visited the main hospital did they gain insight into the challenges that the whole system was facing. By narrowing their focus on what they felt was within their control, the Community Service Centres had overlooked the broader systemic impact of the whole patient experience. Adopting a move towards strategy, they had unknowingly created what they had tried to avoid. The impact was to unintentionally create challenges for their patients and the Trust's Senior Executive team.

The approach to resolving these unintentional challenges was to create safety for open dialogue and exploration across the whole organisational system. In practice, this meant replacing their move towards strategy with 'a move with strategy', an approached based on building mutuality that we will explore in more detail in Chap. 7.

Case Study 4.2 Team: Moving Against Dysfunction
A global retail organisation was becoming increasingly concerned that a large number of transformation programmes were not delivering their intended outcomes. Their change programmes and projects were struggling to meet deadlines, going over budget and failing to deliver tangible results. Not being able to get to root causes of these challenges, the Executive Board decided that the best way forward was to create a new centralised Change Support Team. The purpose of the new function was to support and facilitate the effective delivery of all business-related transformation programmes and projects. Unfortunately, the positive intent at the outset was not met in reality.

The positive intention of providing a resourceful supportive agenda evolved into a governance function in practice. Feeling that they were held to account for facilitating successful outcomes, one of the impacts was the new change team set about taking control of delivery. By introducing new policies, combined with structured project methodologies and communication practices, the new team's focus became aligned to risk reduction. The programme and project managers from within the division who had expected to be supported and empowered by the new team experienced the opposite, feeling unsupported and disempowered. After a four-month period one of the observed outcomes was information sharing being reduced to a need to know basis. Divisional leaders felt entitled to be supported by the new function, and the change team felt entitled to be provided with information, answers and outcomes. The overall impact was a stalemate. Projects were still failing, and this

(continued)

Case Study 4.2 (continued)

time the blame was being laid at the door of the new change function because they were not meeting expectations of providing guidance and support.

The outcome from this unintended challenge was that the Change Support Team sought support to conduct a review of their operational functioning. The result was a detailed analysis of how they utilised and deployed power in their approaches to initiating, building and maintaining client relationships. The utilisation of power in relationships is a topic that we will explore in greater depth in Chap. 6.

Case Study 4.3 Individual: Move Away from Risk

Tom, a leader of a financial trading function, was becoming increasingly concerned that his team focused on working within the boundaries of their existing revenue streams. He could see a whole raft of new revenue potential for exploring different markets. Despite numerous conversations of encouragement, he couldn't understand why a single person had not taken any action. His perception was that people were reluctant to take risks, preferring to focus on what was known and understood.

Exploring the functioning of the team, we uncovered that Tom's perceptions were correct. The reason people were reluctant to take risks with venturing into new and different options and territories was that they did not feel safe. The concept of the team was held in name only. In practice, the team consisted of a group of 17 individuals, each focusing on their own revenue generation streams. The structure of the operational functioning of the team was built on individual accountability and responsibility. There was no concept of 'we' as a team. The focus was on 'I' the individual. Day-to-day interactions consisted of each member having separate one-to-one conversations with Tom. The only person who had a view of the broader business strategy was Tom. The team did not have a collective, clearly defined purpose or agenda. As individuals were personally held to account for their efforts, they were reluctant to take risks for fear of failure. The consequences of making a mistake not only threatened their income, they also felt that their jobs and ultimately careers were at stake. Individual members reported that keeping themselves to themselves seemed like the safest option. By focusing his efforts in what he perceived was providing support to individuals, Tom had overlooked that he had unintentionally contributed to creating a risk-averse fear biased team culture.

Supported by understanding the causes to their challenges Tom and his team embarked on a journey of building a new team focused operating model that facilitated a mutuality partnership based culture. We will return to the practices that contribute to creating mutuality-based environments in greater detail in Chaps. 5 and 6.

Why Is Ambiguity Challenging?

One of the interesting factors about fear, attachment, control and entitlement responses is that they highlight the challenge of the psychological construct of our control biased Western mind-sets. For those of us not at the front line of the armed forces putting our physical lives in danger, fear is not real. In our Western paradigm fear is projected onto a future that is yet to happen. In organisations fear can be projected onto potential loss of income, employment, career advancement and reputation. Attachment is an energetic and psychological construct, as human beings are not physically attached to anything. Despite how much we may want it, the impermanent nature of our universe means that in reality, we can control nothing. Entitlement is constructed around patterns in social norms, we are not entitled to anything, we come into the world with nothing, and we leave it with nothing. The process of linking these realisations with the concept of impermanence evoked questions. Why do we create suffering for ourselves and others in response to a phenomenon that in practice is present in every moment of our existence? The question that drew my intrigue was in an organisational context, why was ambiguity a problem for some leaders and not for others?

Reviewing the different experiences of individuals, teams and organisations, the thread that ran through their challenges was that impermanence generates ambiguity. Ambiguity evokes fear, fear and responses to fear create suffering in some shape or form. Sills (2009) suggests that ambiguity, along with craving and aversion, is at the root of our suffering and challenging experiences. Sills proposes that ambiguity leads to experiences of polarised feelings that show up as positive, negative or neutral responses that arise in relation to a particular experience. Put simply, positive draws good feelings, experiences and active engagement. A negative experience generates unpleasant feelings and/or experiences. Neutral experiences have no positive or negative impact. The more intense the negative or positive feelings and responses, the more polarised the relationship to the experience becomes, which in turn leads to the notion of what we perceive as being good and bad.

Combining these concepts, if we feel good about something, we are likely to engage with it. If we feel bad about something, we are likely not to want to engage, and/or run away from it, and if we feel neutral about something we are likely not to respond or act. Sills suggests that our sense-of-self can be defensive and split. The more challenging the ambiguity experience, the more split and defensive we become.

Building on the notion of defensive splitting within the self, utilising Fairbairn's (1994) object-relations theory Sills proposes that three self-territories emerge the central-self, needy-self and rejecting-self. Territories of self are formed as a consequence of the push-pull responses to our relational experiences (Illustration 4.1).

The central-self organises around the good experience, aspects that are perceived to be good fulfilling, unambiguous and in some sense known. The central-self maintains an idealised self-perspective and how it wishes to be and how it wants others to see and relate to them. What Jung (1976) terms as the shadow aspects of the

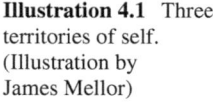

Illustration 4.1 Three territories of self. (Illustration by James Mellor)

central-self are that it holds expectations that others will meet its needs only to be disappointed when the idealised or perceived needs are not matched with reality.

The needy-self is driven by attachment to a desire for fulfilment, organising itself around aspects, and/or people that have the potential to meet its needs. The shadow of the needy-self longs for connectedness and intimacy and yet does not always fully attain it in all circumstances. The rejecting-self organises around the rejecting experience, informed by the frustration and distress generated by the betrayal of unmet or overridden needs.

In summary, the central-self creates the context and standards for the filters of what is good. The needy-self strives to get the good needs met, and the rejecting-self defends the central-self when expectations and ideals are not met.

Working with Ambiguity

Knowing the Self-Self Relationship

One of our Western social traits is that we tend to pay more attention to the relationships we have with others than we do with understanding the nature of the relationships we have with ourselves. Drawing off my own and organisational experiences over the years, I have found that a critical resource for working with ambiguity is knowing the nature of the relationships we have with ourselves. Despite knowing that our bodies are continuously evolving, our psychological disposition has a tendency to perceive itself as being fixed. We create our own inherent ambiguity experiences when we split within ourselves through leaning into how we process and respond to unmet needs. The more ambiguity that we generate for ourselves through our inner processes, the more challenging it is to cope with ambiguity in our environments.

Gaining insight into the nature of our self-self relationship is a useful resource, particularly at times of extreme ambiguity overwhelm. By drawing awareness to the nature of our self-self relationship, we can pause and reflect on our inner experiences, to support us to notice how our responses may be influencing our thinking and behaviour. When we know the symptoms of our inner splitting experiences, we can support ourselves to explore potential causes. This provides us with an opportunity for choice in how we relate to ourselves, others and the broader environment. Which creates a more informed and resourceful approach than simply striving to attain needs and acting out our frustrations, when the world does not meet our expectations.

Knowing Ambiguity Processing Patterns

While supporting leaders to inquire into the nature of the Self-Self relationship with their ambiguity challenges, we discovered that the way they represented their experiences varied. Some leaders used words and phrases that were related to cognitive thinking. For example, disorientated, cannot think straight, unclear, complex, paradoxical, confused, messy, cloudy and dark. Others used words were fear, concern, apprehension, despair and nervousness, responses that were more aligned to emotional responses. There were also the examples of some leaders who described physical symptoms such as energised, stiff, nausea, headaches and tight chest. The range of these different descriptions highlighted that individuals were experiencing ambiguity through what Bandler and Grinder (1979) term as different Representational Systems (Fig. 4.2).

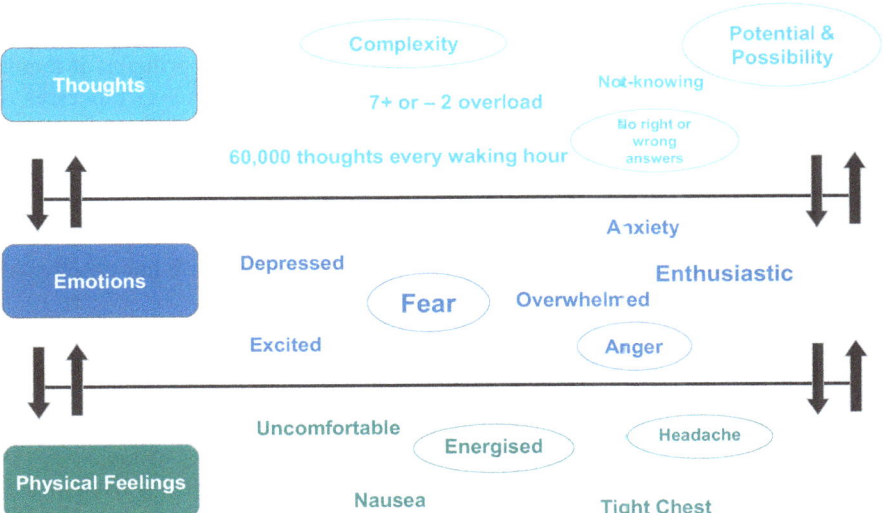

Fig. 4.2 Ambiguity processing patterns

We found that supporting individuals to explore into how they were representing their ambiguous experiences opened the door for awareness, creating opportunities for inquiring into the nature of the Self-Self relationship. For example, some leaders gained insight and understanding from exploring patterns in how they were thinking about their ambiguous challenges. For other leaders, they gained support by inquiring into the triggers that fuelled their emotional responses. While others discovered that exploring what they described as odd physical sensations unveiled and gave access to early warning signs and aspects that their bodies were processing outside of conscious awareness. Regardless of how their ambiguity experiences showed up, having insight into their primary processing patterns facilitated a journey of self-inquiry, exploration and discovery. This reflective self-inquiry process supported leaders to direct their attention inwards. An alternative approach to their natural tendency is to focus their attention on the projective perceived world outside of themselves. We will be illustrating practices for self-inquiry in Chap. 10.

The Impermanent Nature of the Self

Another aspect that drove my curiosity was the transitory shifts in how leaders reported their ambiguous experiences. Some days it would all be too much and complete overwhelm, and on other days the same experience was just annoying or irritating. In a practical sense, nothing of any significance had changed. It was the shifting dimensions in the nature of the relationship that the individuals were having with their challenges that drew another focus for inquiry and exploration.

The Buddhist philosophical concept of the Skandhas provides a helpful perspective for shining light into the continuously evolving complexities of the self-self relationship. Freemantle (2003) proposes that the Skandhas illuminate the impermanent nature of how our sense-of-self is created. The primary principle is that as with our environments, we as human beings are also in continuous processes of transition. There are five Skandhas: form, feeling, perception, conditioning and consciousness. What follows is my interpretation of how they inform the relational experiences with ourselves others and environment.

Form Refers to anything that can be perceived by our senses whether it is sight, smell, touch, hearing and taste. It's how we come into contact with our experiences of something or someone.

Feeling These are the immediate responses to impressions of form both physical and emotional, instinctive sensations that arise as feelings that can be positive, negative or neutral. Our feelings correspond with emotional sensations of happiness, sadness or indifference. In some instances, our feeling responses may not always be fully experienced as intense emotions, they can also operate as a backdrop to thoughts, actions, likes and dislikes.

Perception Relates to knowing that can also be termed as cognition or recognition. Perception is how we relate the present moment to our past experiences and give form and feelings meaning. To see aspects that we have known in the past and how our histories shape what we see, in the present. This whole process makes it possible to label and express our experiences, transforming them into thoughts and words.

Conditioning Relates to values, judgements and historical beliefs about the world, which inform our behaviours and what we predict will happen in the future. Conditioning influences our intentions and where we focus our attention.

Consciousness Is a dynamic process that coordinates how we are seeing and interpreting a situation. In other words, it is how we know what we are knowing. How we are experiencing the inputs from our senses and what we are feeling in any given moment. Our consciousness is the facilitator for attraction and attachment to what is known.

Freemantle proposes that these are interconnected elements that mutually influence and inform each other. Where the Skandhas can help is when we draw awareness to one of these elements, we create the potential for changing our whole experience of a situation. We found that when leaders focused their attention on the different elements of the Skandhas and related them to their ambiguity experiences, they were able to gain more in-depth insight into their self-self relationship. This self-inquiry process supported them to see and understand patterns in their responses that were often out of conscious awareness. By understanding their primary ambiguity processing patterns, leaders were able to draw awareness to how their inner experiences were influencing their leadership behaviours. Many reported utilising their self insights as early warning signals, as prompts to interrupt their rejecting-self, knee jerk reactions and avoid the pull to slip into fight, freeze or flight stress-related responses. In practice, this meant that they were able to bring resources to support themselves and others with their ambiguity challenges.

Skandhas in Organisations

The Skandhas are also a useful framework for illuminating the concept of how organisations are comprised of integrated, interconnected processes of interaction. When using the Skandhas to gain insight into organisations, the same principle applies that when we draw awareness to one of these elements, the potential is created for changing the whole organisational experience. What follows is how the Skandhas are represented in an organisational context.

Form in Organisations Form relates to the shape, physical manifestation and how the organisation works, like structures, working practices, policies and procedures. Form is also experienced in relationships. For example, like the forms of communication that leaders use to relate to their workforces, communication styles that can range from telling, sharing, inquiring and inviting, they all set the tone for the responses that they receive from their recipients.

Feeling in Organisations How feelings are expressed in organisations will influence the workforce, stakeholders and client experiences. For example, this can be the difference between an organisation being an exciting place to work, versus chaotic and overwhelming, where nothing is ever good enough.

Perception in Organisations Create frames and filters of experience. Leaders and their teams will see some aspects of an experience and overlook others because their experiences are filtered through their perceptions. In practice, what they perceive will inform what they create.

Conditioning in Organisations This manifests as the habits and tendencies where leaders and their workforces see what they look for. Conditioning can result in taking for granted and relying on known ways of operating. The outcomes of applying historical success recipes can facilitate overlooking the needs to act differently in the moment, like missing the new industry requirements and emerging market trends.

Consciousness in Organisations Relates to what is known that informs patterns in thinking, behaviour and operational functioning. The attachment to known ways of working can often be labelled as 'resistance to change'. Embracing new and different alternatives can often become clouded and informed by what is known that it becomes challenging to fully leverage the creative potential and opportunities of the unknown.

Case studies 4.4, 4.5 and 4.6 illustrate how the principles of the Skandhas were utilised to provide insight and facilitate constructive transitions for case studies 4.1, 4.2 and 4.3.

Case Study 4.4 Expressing Feelings in Community Services
When the Community Services of the Healthcare Trust drew awareness to their feelings of disempowerment and became conscious of how this related to the patient experience, it opened up the doorway for collective dialogue. Where both parties could explore and understand the differences in their experiences. The outcome created a supportive context to explore the split and disconnected aspects of the combined functioning of their organisations in relationships, processes, policies and procedures.

Case Study 4.5 Forms of Engagement in Retail Change Team
By gaining insight into the impact of their known control biased forms of engagement, the retail change team became conscious of their unintended consequences. They provided themselves with the opportunity to understand how, despite their positive intentions they were unknowingly getting in the way of successful programme and project delivery. The team uncovered informative insights that created the potential for new practices and forms of engagement to be developed to fulfil their purpose and support the organisation as a whole.

Case Study 4.6 Conditioned Perceptions of Tom
When Tom became aware of his conditioned perceptions of his individual biased leadership style, he could see how he had unknowingly created a risk-averse fear-based culture. His insights opened up the potential for him to learn how to develop a new team focused operating model that facilitated an integrated partnership focused culture.

Organisational Politics

The collective impact of ambiguity anxiety and the interrelated dynamics of the different processing strategies inform what is generally termed as politics in organisations. The more split and ambiguous our inner experiences, the more challenged we are to deal with inherent ambiguity in our environments. It is an aspect that highlights the principle that impermanence is an inner and outer construct of our living world experiences. In the context of transitions, impermanence relates to our through-time relationship with the transitional journey, and it also aligns with the momentary in-time relationship we have with our transition experiences. Having an orientation of the transitional space and the through-time journey helps and yet when we do not have insight into the nature of our self-self relationship we can still get in our own way and ultimately the functioning of organisations.

We cannot tick the box and say that we can make ourselves immune from ambiguity because it will appear in some shape or form depending on the transitional context. The key factor is knowing when ambiguity is present and drawing awareness to the impact that it is having on our inner self construct experiences, patterns of thinking, emotional and physical states of being at the time. In a transitional leadership context, it is about knowing the impact of ambiguity and how our responses influence our behaviour and relationships with our environment. Key aspects that are always present in our daily-lived experiences in organisations that have a tendency for being overlooked or taken for granted.

Unfortunately, politics = dysfunction in organisations, a critical factor that makes coping and working with environments of continuous change even more challenging. As we have been exploring, it is difficult to navigate complex change in our environments, when our inner self constructs are split and disconnected. The same applies to organisations when overwhelmed with their ambiguous inner experiences they are challenged to work with and embrace the opportunities that a continuously evolving landscape provides.

When we do not understand the levels of complexity that inform responses to ambiguity anxiety, we can be quick to judge and respond, particularly when we are on the receiving end of it. Although, when we develop an understanding that dysfunctional behaviours are derived from stress-related responses, we can be more forgiving. Compassion for dysfunctional behaviour is more natural when having an understanding of the factors that might be informing and driving it, shining a light into the complex dynamics of our human nature. Compassion for fear-driven responses supports us to remind ourselves that ambiguity is part of our world experiences and present for all of us regardless of our different tolerance levels. Knowing these core principles of our human functioning also highlights the importance and requirement of self-compassion. Without compassion for ourselves, it is difficult to provide and hold it for others. Particularly in circumstances when we are sharing the same experience, and others are having responses and reactions that are different from our own. Holding compassion is a key and essential transition leadership practice that we will explore along with other resourceful practices in the following chapters.

Summary

What we have been exploring in this chapter is that ambiguity is naturally present in some shape or form in all of our day-to-day lived experiences. It is the nature of the different relationships we have with our ambiguous experiences that is the difference that makes the difference, particularly when it comes to successfully navigating transitions in organisations. The key principles are that there are two core factors for working with ambiguity. First, knowing patterns in our self-self relationship with ambiguity and how these inform our experiences of transitions. Second, it is also about knowing how our combined lived experiences, inform how we respond and react when ambiguous circumstances make an appearance.

An Invitation for Self-Inquiry
To ground the concepts of this chapter in applied practice, the invitation is to return to draw awareness to your own transition experience. Here are a few questions to support your inquiry:

Relationships with Ambiguity
Ambiguity – where is this present in your current transition experience?
Representation – how is your ambiguity experience showing up? (thoughts, emotions, physical symptoms)
Context – what requirements/needs are informing your ambiguity experiences?
Responses – how are your inner experiences influencing your behaviour?
FACE – are any responses related to fear, attachment, control or entitlement?
Derailers – are there any move towards, against or away strategies present?
Impact – if so, how might these be informing your relationships with self/others?
Insight – what insights have you gained about your current transition experience?

Exploring Repeating Patterns
In addition to exploring immediate experiences with ambiguity, I have found that it is also helpful to gain insights into repeating patterns so that we can pre-empt and catch them when they arrive. Knowing our primary ambiguity processing patterns can give us a heads up on contexts or scenarios that can trigger and lead to unconscious responses. Having these insights about our primary processing patterns provides us with informed choices of how we are engaging and responding to different ambiguity experiences as our transitional journeys evolve.

1. Are any of the above representations, situations and/or responses familiar?
2. If so, in what contexts, situations, scenarios or relationships do they appear?
3. Are there any common threads in the outcomes that your patterns generate?
4. What impact does having insight into your repeating patterns have?
5. How might these inform your relationship with ambiguity, self/others and leadership practices going forward?

As with the previous exercises, if you have more of your own questions, please include them. Self-inquiry and reflection are key capabilities for working with ambiguity. The more we explore and inquire into our experiences, particularly how they relate to the nature of our self-self relationship, the greater the range of resources, options and potential we can generate both for ourselves and organisations.

It will be helpful to record your responses as we will build on these in the next chapters.

(continued)

References

Bandler, R., & Grinder, J. (1979). *Frogs into princes. The introduction to neuro-linguistic programming*. London: Eden Grove Editions.

Fairbairn, R. (1994). In E. Birtles & D. Sharff (Eds.), *Clinical and theoretical papers. Vol I of from instinct to self: Selected papers of W. R. D Fairbairn*. London/Northvale: Jason Aronson.

Freemantle, F. (2003). *Luminous emptiness. Understanding the Tibetan book of the dead*. Boston: Shambhala.

Hanson, R. (2009). *The practical neuroscience of Buddha's brain happiness, love & wisdom*. Raincoast Books: New Harbinger Publications, Inc.

Hogan, R., & Hogan, J. (2001). Assessing leadership: A view of the dark side. *International Journal of Selection and Assessment, 9*, 40–51.

Horney, K. (1950). *Neurosis and human growth*. New York: Norton.

Jung, C. G. (1976). *The development of personality. Vol. 17 of the collected works of C G Jung*. Princeton: Princeton University Press.

Levine, P. A. (1997). *Waking the Tiger. Healing trauma*. Berkley: North Atlantic Books.

Richo, D. (2006). *The five things we cannot change and the happiness we find by embracing them*. Boulder: Shambhala Publications.

Siegel D J (2010) The mindful therapist. New YorkNorton and Company.

Sills, F. (2009). *Being and becoming*. Berkeley: North Atlantic Books.

Part II
Transition Leadership

In Part I, we illuminated the complex dynamics and approaches for working with the in-time and through-time experiences of the transitional space. Chapters 5, 6, 7 and 8 explore the different territories of effective Transition Leadership practices. Resourceful leadership approaches that support individuals, teams and organisations navigate and work with the complex dimensions of continuously changing environments.

Chapter 5
Self-Insight

Introduction

In this chapter, we will be building on the journey we began in Part 1, deepening insight into the principle of knowing the Self in a transition leadership context. It explores why the process of drawing awareness to unseen and overlooked aspects of our human being dimensions is a core resource to support effective transition leadership practices. It reveals practical sustainable approaches for gaining awareness and insight into factors that influence and inform what successful transition leaders do and how they approach their leadership agendas. We begin the journey by exploring the different types of transitions that inform the evolution of a successful leadership career path and share the research findings of how core capabilities influence preferences and create unseen patterns in leadership practices. It also highlights the concept that when core capabilities are understood, the insights obtained can inform the way that leaders approach and work with their transitional challenges.

Contextual Transitions of Leadership Practices

Technical knowledge is considered to be a core-contributing factor to the effectiveness of organisations. Leaders are frequently promoted on the depth of their knowledge and how they apply their technical expertise. A factor that is often overlooked is that in the process of developing leadership skills and knowledge, the context of responsibility, focus of delivery, and where leaders focus their attention is an evolving process. What goes unseen is that practically developing a leadership career requires working with increasing levels of complexity. There is also the requirement to integrate contextual shifts in thinking and behaviour that inform where leaders direct the focus of their attention (Fig. 5.1).

© Springer Nature Switzerland AG 2020
C. Hayes, *Transition Leadership*, https://doi.org/10.1007/978-3-030-42787-0_5

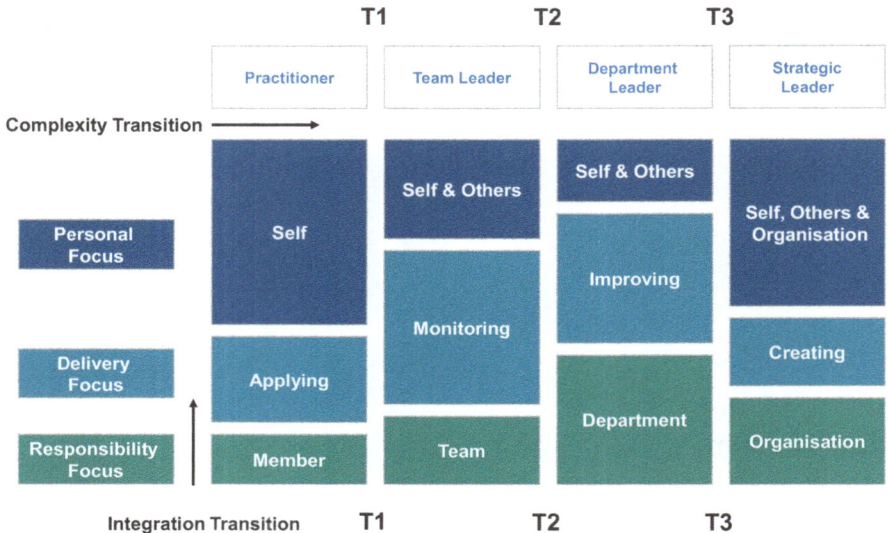

Fig. 5.1 Leadership career transitions

T1: Transition

As we begin the career journey as practitioners, our frames-of-reference are Self-orientated. Our focus of delivery is directed towards acquiring and integrating knowledge and skills, applying what we have learned to deliver results in line with specified tasks. Our responsibilities are focused on participating as a member of a team, contributing to the achievement of team goals and supporting fellow team colleagues. Typically what happens at the beginning of a leadership career is that when practitioners do well with integrating and applying these different aspects to achieve outcomes, they are offered promotion to become a team leader. As team leaders embrace the responsibilities of their new roles, they are immediately faced with the contextual shift of the T1 Transition.

Navigating the T1 Transition requires a shift in the delivery focus. It is a new transitional journey from focusing on the Self, delivering tasks to supporting and monitoring the work of individuals, while building and maintaining the effective collective functioning of a team. In practice there becomes an increase in the complexities of role requirements. The responsibilities that team leaders are being held to account for are how they support and facilitate others to deliver outcomes.

The focus of attention becomes orientated around the functioning and performance of the team. The core team leadership tasks are setting and monitoring performance standards, facilitating and supporting the individuals and the team as a whole to deliver outcomes in line with functional purpose and objectives. There are also the added responsibilities of participating as members of other functional teams.

The personal development agenda of a team leader is to acquire insight into preferences, motivations and an understanding of how their leadership approaches impact and influence others. It requires enhancing communication skills and developing approaches for building effective relationships and understanding the interconnected dynamics of team functioning. In practice, the transition from practitioner to team leader introduces a contextual shift in frame-of-reference. It requires integrating the practice of leading others, into the day-to-day operational focus of the Self. The development focus of team leaders is acquiring new skills and knowledge to develop the capabilities for working with complexities of an increased level of responsibility.

T2: Transition

As team leaders integrate the skills, knowledge and practicalities of supporting and building effective teams, the next contextual challenge is the T2 Transition, as they undertake the role of department leader.

Navigating the T2 Transition requires shifting the delivery focus from one team to leading the effective functioning of multiple teams, in order to contribute to a broader organisational agenda. The added complexities of role requirements are focused around continuous improvement of delivery and services. Continually questioning what is being achieved, introducing and encouraging new/different ideas, and the improvement of processes and systems. The practical delivery focus is on developing and implementing strategies, to improve the effectiveness of services and outputs of a functional department. The personal leadership context is on the Self as being the leader of other team leaders in a broader organisational context.

The focus of responsibility requires creating and reviewing department performance targets in line with organisational purpose and strategies. In practice, this requires creating and providing resources to support the department to achieve its purpose and defined objectives. Department leadership also requires supporting and facilitating the development, transitions and transformation of leaders, teams and the department as a whole. While simultaneously participating as members of a broad range of different teams and agendas to sponsor and support the contributions that the department makes to the broader organisation.

The personal development focus of a department leader centres on acquiring a range of different leadership styles, to provide options and greater flexibility in facilitative approaches. In practice this requires deploying a range of sophisticated problem-solving techniques to work with multifaceted aspects of complexity, not-knowing and ambiguity. In addition, it also requires enhancing the leadership capacity to work with multifaceted challenges to facilitate productive relationships and build sustainable partnerships. The frame-of-reference shift from team to department leader centres on creating contexts of improvement for the department and contributing to the functioning of the broader organisational agenda.

T3: Transition

As department leaders become proficient and deepen their skills for developing and implementing performance improvement strategies, the next contextual shift is the T3 Transition. In practice, it requires a new contextual shift for embracing strategic leadership accountabilities.

Navigating the T3 Transition requires shifting the focus of delivery to developing and leading organisation-wide strategies. This means facilitating transformational approaches that create purpose and directional focus for the organisation as a whole. In large organisations, strategic leadership practices are also required for leading divisions of multiple departments. The increased complexities of role requirements are focused on the effective functioning of the organisation and the practical delivery focus is targeted at connectivity and integration. In practice strategic leadership requires fostering a performance culture and operational environment that aligns the organisation with evolving industry and market trends while seeking opportunities for innovation. The primary leadership focus is on creating and facilitating the development of partnerships with internal and external parties. The personal leadership emphasis is centred on the Self, being the representative leader of the organisation in the broader market and industry environment.

The development agenda of a strategic leader focuses on personal impact and the utilisation of their strategic position for supporting and improving the organisation. It requires developing capabilities for designing and building long-term strategic agendas, returning authority and encouraging engagement and active participation from the workforce. Strategic leaders find themselves faced with learning how to utilise power through co-creating and facilitating cultures based on integrated partnerships. The roles of strategic leaders are on full view to the organisation's workforce and external stakeholders. In practice this makes a call on the leader to have depth of self-insight, emotional intelligence and personal resilience practices. The shift in frame-of-reference from department to strategic leader centres around the leader being the living ambassador of the organisational values and performance standards for the workforce and external stakeholders.

Aligning Behaviours with Leadership Contexts

Leaders report that when they have insight into the evolution of the different contextual shifts, in frames-of-reference, it provides clarity of focus. Providing a clearly defined frame-of-reference that facilitates insight into the types of activities, fundamental knowledge and skills that their roles require. New team leaders also report that it illuminates the different leadership territories and the kinds of transitions that they may need to navigate to enhance and develop their careers over time.

A common challenge I experience in organisations is that leaders find themselves in senior leadership positions with mismatched skills and knowledge, discovering that their frames-of-reference and practices are out of context with what their leadership roles require. For example, like James in Chap. 3 (case study 3.1) spending the whole of his career becoming a technology specialist. James instantly found himself faced with having to navigate the T1, T2 and T3 transitional shifts to embrace the responsibilities and accountabilities of being the strategic leader of a new division. There is also the example of Tom, the team leader from Chap. 4, (case study 4.3) who was trying to lead a global trading team informed by the practitioner frame-of-reference. Tom experienced the unintended consequences of not acquiring and developing team leadership skills that resulted in creating a risk-averse fear-based culture.

Both of these leaders were highly skilled, capable professionals; their challenges were created by not knowing what they did not know about the context of their leadership responsibilities. Once these leaders had insight into the different leadership contexts and the specific practices required for their roles, they were able to acquire the necessary skills and knowledge to be effective, impactful leaders. Leaders who continued to develop and broaden their careers by taking on more senior strategic roles and making significant contributions to their organisations.

Leaders of Thought

Many leaders of today class themselves as specialists and experts. They perceive themselves as leaders of thought who focus their attention on applying their technical knowledge and skills to achieve specified outcomes. The emphasis of their work is related to assembling teams to deliver specialised or specific targeted projects. When their programmes and projects are completed, the teams are disbanded, and specialist resources are redeployed on to other projects. The leaders of programme and project teams tend to deploy their leadership responsibilities from the context of practitioners because they consider themselves to be accountable for the delivery of specified business outcomes. As opposed to department or strategic leaders who are responsible for the on-going development and effectiveness of operational teams.

Although as we have been exploring in Part 1, honouring complexity and working with inherent ambiguities are core practices for successful delivery of organisation transformations. Regardless of purpose or duration, delivering successful project outcomes can be significantly enhanced when leaders create and hold the context of supportive environments. Supportive environments unite the capabilities and efforts of individual team members to co-create effective consolidated project outcomes. Delivering successful projects can be incredibly challenging experiences if leaders have not navigated their way through the T1 transitional journey, as we explored with the example of the regulatory project team in Chap. 3 (case study 3.2).

Another aspect that I frequently see in organisations is the absence of expertise driven thought leadership career paths. I meet many specialist programme and project leaders who have walked the pathway of undertaking operational team leadership roles because they see no alternative options for enhancing their careers. The underlying belief in these leaders is that the only way they can increase their earning potential is to take on a more senior organisational leadership role. In those instances, I have found that the leadership transitions framework can be utilised to create opportunities for exploration and dialogue. When leaders gain an understanding of the different leadership contexts and the types of transitions that they will be required to navigate, it facilitates informed choice about the direction of travel in their careers. I have worked with many strategic leaders who recognised that they were walking the wrong career pathway, either by accident or by choice. These individuals were able to utilise the leadership transitions framework to explore and create new thought leadership career pathways, many undertaking new roles within their existing organisations.

Leadership Transitions

The core principle that we have been illuminating is that leading successful transitions in organisations requires leaders to navigate the development of their own transitional journeys. In practice, this means knowing and understanding the different stages of leadership development and the different types of transitions that support effective practices and outcomes. The difference is that successful transition leaders know the context of the leadership role, where to focus their attention and the types of behaviours and activities that facilitate effective outcomes for themselves, others and organisations. When leaders have insight into the different contextual shifts and territories of role requirements, they can mitigate the risk of creating unnecessary complexity and ambiguity for themselves and others. Leaders become able to create opportunities for closing skills and knowledge gaps, enhancing their personal effectiveness in existing roles, taking proactive steps towards creating a pathway for future career development.

Core Capabilities

Exploring the different dimensions of ambiguity processing patterns and responses, I became intrigued about the leaders that were excelling with their change and transformation challenges. My curiosity led to an inquiry into the practices of 200 successful leaders, across a range of different business functions (operations, technology, sales, finance, compliance and human resources). Analysing information obtained from interviews and focus groups with successful leaders and their teams one of the key findings was that there were distinct patterns that informed their leadership working practices.

What we uncovered were four core capabilities: production, project, relationship and expert. Each capability had a specific core purpose that contributed to the effective functioning of the organisation (Fig. 5.2).

Fig. 5.2 Core capabilities

Production Maintains the operational infrastructure and the requirement for consistently repeated processes, procedures and policies.

Project Designs, plans and implements transformations that inform the current and future requirements of the organisation.

Relationship Connects people to share information across boundaries and disciplines with internal, external parties and the broader environment.

Expert Utilises specialist knowledge and skills to contribute to the core functioning and purpose of the organisation.

We found that core capabilities related to two aspects of the leadership role: the type of work that was conducted and how the leaders deployed their responsibilities. What became known as primary and secondary core capabilities.

Primary Capabilities

Primary capabilities inform the type of work that leaders perform and the key responsibilities of their day-to-day activities. We found that there were synergies between primary core capabilities and functional operational requirements in organisations. For example, production aligned with operational and distribution functions. Project related to responsibilities for implementing change, including programme management activities. Relationship aligned to sales and any type of internal/external client relational activities. Expert informed the requirements for depth in specialist technical knowledge and skills that covered a broad range of business needs, like technology, law, human resources and finance.

Secondary Capabilities

Secondary capabilities inform how leaders approach their leadership responsibilities, these can be the same or different to primary capabilities. For example, the role of a relationship orientated leader responsible for leading change within a sales function is greatly supported by the secondary capability of project. Alternatively, for an expert lawyer responsible for leading and developing the effectiveness of a specialist division, the secondary capabilities of production were useful resources.

Evolving Capabilities

We found that there were no fixed patterns in how these primary or secondary capabilities are formed. For some leaders, they were directly aligned to personalities and their choice of career path. For others, core capabilities were formed by the evolution of their careers. One of the interesting findings was that primary capabilities tend to sustain themselves over time. It was the secondary capabilities that tended to shift as leaders took on new responsibilities and developed their careers. Case study 5.1 illustrates how the secondary capabilities evolved through the transitional development of my career.

Case Study 5.1 Cath's Evolving Capability Journey
I began my career in the field of Training and Development because I wanted to contribute to supporting the effectiveness of organisations, through enhancing the skills and knowledge of people. The nature of my work in the mid-1980s focused on supporting individuals to acquire and develop new skills and knowledge. My day-to-day responsibilities were focused on teaching knowledge and skills development programmes that were facilitated by the primary and secondary capabilities of relationship. Over time as my career evolved into the field of Organisation Development, the nature of my work centred on initiating and running transformation programmes and projects. As a result, the secondary capabilities for how I conducted my work became Project. After switching my full-time career into consulting the focus of my work centred around supporting organisations to work with and solve complex transition challenges. Over 12 years of consulting the impact on my secondary capabilities have evolved into Expert.

Since uncovering the core capabilities and how they inform leadership practices, I have experienced cases where drawing awareness to primary and secondary capabilities supported leaders, to make dramatic shifts in their career paths. These leaders citing that the reasons that they were feeling unfulfilled in their work was because their roles were not in line with their primary and/or secondary capabilities. These individuals recognised that they were following a path that no longer motivated them or that they had unknowingly made some inappropriate choices at different stages of their career journeys.

Core Capabilities and Ambiguity

Another useful discovery that emerged from the research was that core capabilities influence the nature of the relationships and responses that individuals have to ambiguity. We found that different capabilities had distinct approaches for working with ambiguity. When it came to effective practices for honouring complexity and working with ambiguity, the key success factors were the alignment of the leaders preferred approach with the specific characteristics of their challenges. Individuals found that they suffered from symptoms of ambiguity anxiety when their preferred tried and tested approaches were out of alignment with the practical characteristics of their challenges. The ambiguity anxiety trigger was the inability to achieve desired outcomes because they could not meet the specific needs that underpinned their preferred approaches.

Production Approach to Ambiguity

Production capabilities work with ambiguity by following a structured process. The focus for production capabilities is on containing ambiguity, setting clear boundaries and approaching transitions as distinct individual events. The preferred transition leadership approach is facilitating incremental change within a known context. The need to be able to see a clearly defined pathway and follow a structured process is a core need for production capabilities. If the pathway ahead is unclear and ambiguous, the impact is projected fear of not-knowing where to start or how to proceed.

Project Approach to Ambiguity

Project capabilities work with ambiguity to meet goals that contribute to achieving clearly defined outcomes. The focus for project capabilities is on exploring the different dimensions of ambiguity, utilising methods and resources that can contribute to meeting requirements in order to deliver outcomes. Having a clearly defined purpose and the abilities to choose and utilise resources are core needs for project capabilities. If goals are unclear or resources cannot be fully utilised, the ambiguity anxiety trigger and projected fear is not-knowing what or how to deliver.

Relationship Approach to Ambiguity

Relationship capabilities work with ambiguity by seeing and forming systemic connections. The focus for relationship capabilities is on acknowledging ambiguity, and working with the complexities of competing tensions to allow the direction of travel to emerge, by creating integrated systems. Being able to connect concepts with different views and alternative perspectives are core needs for relationship capabilities. If relationships are difficult to form or there is a lack of interest in dialogue the projected fear is that core factors will be unseen, overlooked and this will have a detrimental impact on the delivery of effective outcomes.

Expert Approach to Ambiguity

Expert capabilities like to utilise knowledge and skills to solve problems and create solutions. The focus for expert capabilities is to seek, remove or work around ambiguity to contribute to the effectiveness of the business agenda. Being able to understand the causes and get to the bottom of complex challenges are core needs for expert capabilities. If solutions cannot be found and resolved, the projected fear is that the optimum outcomes cannot be achieved (Fig. 5.3).

While each capability has a different approach for leading transitions and working with ambiguity, individually and collectively, they can all make valuable contributions to organisations. The key contributory factor is when core capabilities are in alignment with the requirements of the business agenda. At first glance, it may look like relationship capabilities have the upper hand when it comes to working with

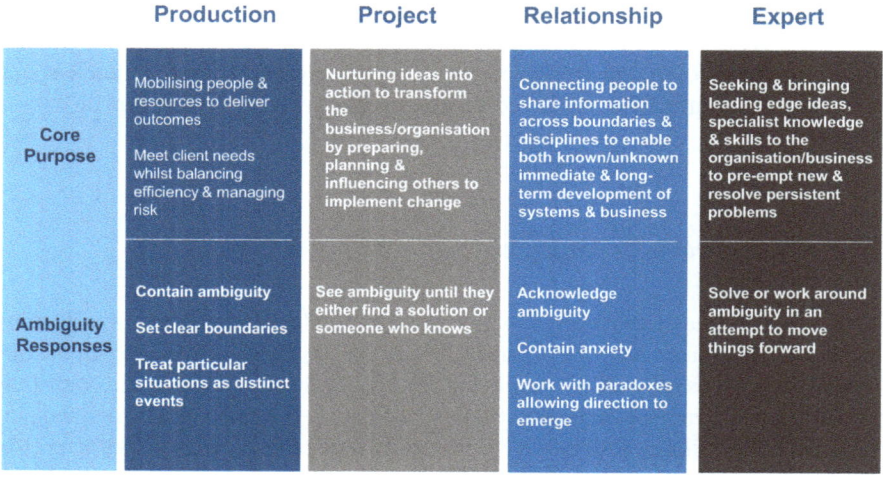

	Production	**Project**	**Relationship**	**Expert**
Core Purpose	Mobilising people & resources to deliver outcomes Meet client needs whilst balancing efficiency & managing risk	Nurturing ideas into action to transform the business/organisation by preparing, planning & influencing others to implement change	Connecting people to share information across boundaries & disciplines to enable both known/unknown immediate & long-term development of systems & business	Seeking & bringing leading edge ideas, specialist knowledge & skills to the organisation/business to pre-empt new & resolve persistent problems
Ambiguity Responses	Contain ambiguity Set clear boundaries Treat particular situations as distinct events	See ambiguity until they either find a solution or someone who knows	Acknowledge ambiguity Contain anxiety Work with paradoxes allowing direction to emerge	Solve or work around ambiguity in an attempt to move things forward

Fig. 5.3 Core capability ambiguity responses

ambiguity. Although this is not necessarily the case, as it depends on the nature of the transition process and change agenda that they are trying to lead.

For example, in instances where there is a need for a focused, incremental approach, relationship capabilities can often be accused of over complicating the task in hand. The tendency is to get too many people involved because of their needs to want to explore, involve and include a range of different perspectives and options. Whereas, project capabilities can often be accused of not knowing when to stop and making the task bigger than it needs to be. Production capabilities can be prone to tunnel vision, unable to see systemic connections and the broader picture. The impact is that production capabilities become challenged with honouring complexity, *'only seeing what they look'*. Whilst expert capabilities tend to seek perfection, focusing on getting to the bottom of solving every problem, for example, like the example of the regulatory project team in Chap. 3 (case study 3.2).

Aligning Capabilities with Business Requirements

Inquiring into the experiences of 50 challenged leaders from a range of different business disciplines, we uncovered a common, consistent thread. At the heart of their challenges was the misalignment with the nature of the leadership role with key core capabilities. By emphasising technical knowledge and skills, what had been overlooked were the core primary and secondary core capabilities required to support effective execution. The difference that seemed to make the difference was aligning the responsibilities of the leadership role with the appropriate core capabilities. Case study 5.2 illustrates what happens when there is a misalignment with role and business requirements and core capabilities.

> **Case Study 5.2 Ralph's Offshore Challenge**
> Ralph was a highly respected leader of a Financial Operations Division. He had a 20-year track record of creating robust operational infrastructures that made significant contributions to the efficiencies and performance of the bank's trade settlement processes. Ralph was so well respected for his capabilities that he was asked to lead the creation of a new offshore operations division. Five months into his new role, Ralph was struggling to translate plans into practice. The new office buildings were three months behind schedule, and the technology infrastructure could not be implemented. These outcomes influenced Ralph's ability to recruit a new local workforce because there was no physical building or infrastructure to accommodate them. Despite, working 15-hour days and weekends, Ralph struggled to join up the dots and gain any traction. Time was ticking away, costs were increasing and Ralph did not know where to turn. Ralph became challenged to coordinate the

(continued)

Case Study 5.2 (continued)

activities of different technical disciplines that were required to complete the new building. His relationships with head office were starting to become fraught and fragmented because of his slipping timelines. Ralph had also overlooked the number of new connections and relationships that he needed to create and maintain to support effective delivery. What started as an exciting venture of creating something new at the outset had turned into a living nightmare.

Ralph's successful track record had been built on having depth of expertise in operational functioning, supported by utilising robust structured approaches for making continuous incremental improvements. Ralph's core capabilities were primary Expert and secondary Production. What Ralph or the Senior Executives who had appointed him into the role had not realised was that the core capability requirements for the role were Project/Relationship. In practice, Ralph had been given a blank piece of paper, the normal state of affairs for the start-up of new projects. Relationship was the core capability required to create and facilitate partnerships with different suppliers, contractors and maintain effective relationships with head office.

Ralph's challenges were created by his primary and secondary capabilities being out of alignment with the requirements of his new leadership role. Ralph was seen as a successful leader of change and yet what Ralph and the senior executives had not seen was that his approach was based on facilitating incremental change within a known structured environment. Ralph had deployed the skills and knowledge that had made him successful for 20 years, although following and applying structured methods was a challenge when they had yet to be created.

Another classic example of this is in sales roles. The core primary or secondary capabilities that create effective sales outcomes are based on relationship. Relationship capabilities build depth in relationship with their clients and seek to find solutions to meet their needs. They also create and facilitate partnerships with their fellow colleagues. The combined outcome is that over time, the sales force gain insights into the different types of products that may be of interest to their clients. Through building depth in relationship with their clients, they learn to see the world from the client's perspective. They know the types of products and services that may be of interest to their clients and as a result, know how to align and develop new products accordingly. If production capabilities are utilised to conduct sales roles, then the outcomes tend to be transactional relationships. Where a structured approach is followed or a script is read out that delivers the subliminal message of *"I have got one of these do you want it or not"*. How often do any of us purchase or do repeat business with people who are just trying to sell us any old product, regardless of our requirements?

Building on Diltz's (1990) concept of logical levels, I discovered that core capabilities underpin behaviours that inform how skills and knowledge are deployed. Core capabilities are the underlying structure that directs the focus of attention and the associated behaviours for how responsibilities are carried out. If core capabilities are out of alignment with business and role requirements, then this will have a direct impact on the outcomes.

Role and capability alignment does not just impact the effectiveness of individual leaders. It also impacts the functioning of teams and organisations like the example of the regulatory project team in Chap. 3. The team required a combination of project, expert and relationship capabilities to support effective delivery. Although in practice, what they had unintentionally created was an expert/expert team. An outcome facilitated by a logical frame-of-reference of focusing on the requirement for expert technical knowledge and skills, to meet complex regulatory requirements.

The same challenge applies to whole organisations. I have worked with many organisations where a concentration of the same core capabilities can unintentionally create fixed patterns in operational functioning. Unseen patterns that inform the culture and can often lock the whole organisation into fixed set ways of working. Executives often finding themselves challenged to navigate continuously changing environments when their primary capabilities are unbalanced and unable to utilise the benefits of integrating all four.

Capability Mapping

Misalignment of core capabilities is a challenge, although it can quickly be resolved. The key success factor is for leaders to have insight into the core capabilities required for the functioning of their business agendas. When leaders combine these insights with an understanding of their own primary/secondary capabilities, they know how to align them with the leadership task in hand. Misalignment is not the end of the world as long as leaders have insight and access to the capabilities that they need to match business requirements to facilitate effective outcomes. As we saw in Chap. 3, once the leader of the regulatory project team understood the core challenge of his project, he was able to take immediate action. All it took to rectify his team's challenges was to deploy primary project and secondary relationship capabilities to fill in the gaps that were missing and explain the principles of the skills and knowledge that were missing to his team.

Leaning into the 'knowledge is power' principle, resourcing and recruiting purely on skills and knowledge is a challenge that I frequently see repeated in organisations. What the core capability research has revealed is that skills and knowledge are only parts of the picture. I have found that high performing leaders, teams and organisations utilise all four capabilities. They know how the concentrations of core capabilities contribute to effective operational functioning and the patterns and traits that inform their cultures. Organisations that follow these principles believe that skills and knowledge can be trained, the key determining factors that underpin successful outcomes for them is core capability, role and business functioning alignment.

When it comes to navigating transitions, successful leaders who utilise capability mapping know their strengths and edges, particularly when it comes to preferred approaches for transition leadership practices and working with ambiguity. In practice, this supports the process of providing informed choice to be able to take proactive actions at the outset of a transformation process. These insights support leaders to pre-empt requirements for additional resources, and they are able to compensate for any gaps that are likely to appear as their transitional journeys evolve.

Capability mapping supports leaders, teams and organisations to build sustainable integrated infrastructures, where they can utilise their insights to inform business planning, recruitment, development, talent and performance management processes. With aligned and integrated infrastructures they find that they can leverage the value of collective diverse capabilities. This in turn facilitates their organisation's abilities to navigate transitions, to work with complexity, foster creativity and innovation. Leaders know what resources they will need in the short and long term and how these will vary and evolve in line with their espoused strategies and changing business environments.

Summary

In this chapter, we have focused on deepening insight into knowing the Self in a transition leadership context. Shining light into the concept that leading successful transitions requires leaders to navigate the development of their own transitional journeys. We have explored the concept of why knowing the context of the leadership role, the focus of attention and the types of behaviours and activities can facilitate effective outcomes. These factors have been supported by the concept of how knowing primary and secondary capabilities can provide insights for leaders, teams and organisations to identify how to align, utilise and deploy their resources. How in practice these combined principles represent key resources for supporting leaders to mitigate the risks of creating unnecessary complexity and ambiguity for themselves and their organisations.

An Invitation for Self-Inquiry

To ground these concepts in application, the invitation is to explore your own current leadership context and the core capabilities that are informing your practice. Here are a few questions to support your inquiry:

Your Current Leadership Context

1. As you reflect on the leadership transitions framework, which context (practitioner, team, department, strategic leader) reflects your current role?

2. What career path (organisation/thought leader) are you on at present?
3. How do your current activities and behaviours align to that context?
4. Are there any skills or knowledge gaps in your current role?
5. If so, what development activities can you undertake to close those gaps?
6. What is the next transition that you are likely to face?
7. What activities can you start doing now to prepare for that transition?
8. What new skills, knowledge do you want to acquire to support your transition?
9. What impact does understanding your current/future leadership contexts have?

Your Core Capabilities

Primary – what capabilities best align with your current role and responsibilities?

Secondary – what capability aligns with how you approach and conduct your work?

Outcomes – how do your capabilities inform your leadership practice?

Needs – what primary requirements inform your approach to ambiguity?

Responses – how do your needs influence your behaviours when they are not met?

Impact – how do your capabilities inform your transition experiences?

Alignment – are there any gaps between your capabilities and your role requirements?

Support – if gaps do exist, what resources can you engage to fill them?

Future – how do your capabilities align with your desired future career path?

Note 5.1
For this inquiry exercise, you may find it helpful to compare review your answers with your notes from Part 1.

Note 5.2
The range of inquiry approaches and methods that informed the core capability research are presented in Part III Chap. 8.

Reference

Dilts, R. (1990). *Changing belief systems with NLP*. Capitola: Meta Publications.

Chapter 6
Team Transitions

Introduction

One of the benchmarks of a leader's performance is the effective functioning and outputs of their teams. And yet, the knowledge, skills and practices required for developing high performing teams can be frequently underestimated and often overlooked.

Developing and sustaining the performance of teams is not as simple as recruiting individual members and calling them a team. A common belief held in today's organisations is that time will be the facilitator of effective team performance. The underpinning principle is that longer people are together the more they will learn to evolve into becoming a high performing team. Unfortunately, this principle is not that straightforward in practice, one of the best worse-case scenarios from this principle is creating teams consisting of individual contributors with their own personal agendas and goals. Alternatively, in the worst-case scenarios, the unintended outcomes can be the formation of dysfunctional low performing teams. The effective functioning of teams can have significant impacts on operational performance and bottom-line outcomes in commercial organisations.

This chapter reveals the core leadership practices that contribute to creating, facilitating and supporting the development of productive high performing teams. Practical approaches that are derived from 15 years of research into the practices of high and low performing teams, across a range of different industries.

Developing high performing teams challenges leaders to develop a practice for understanding and working within the transitional territories of three key aspects:

1. Stages of team development
2. Flexibility of leadership styles
3. Conflict-handling approaches

The following topics provide insights into why these aspects are essential and applied practical approaches for working with them.

© Springer Nature Switzerland AG 2020
C. Hayes, *Transition Leadership*, https://doi.org/10.1007/978-3-030-42787-0_6

Stages of Team Development

Developing and maintaining the effective performance of teams requires an invest-ment of time and effort, from leaders and the team as a whole. The primary reason is that teams are continuously evolving through various transitional stages of devel-opment. There is a vast amount of research and literature about the development of teams. The work of Wheelan (2005) has been the most closely aligned with my own discoveries, of team transitional processes over the years. As with Tuckman's (1965) original model (forming, storming, norming, performing), Wheelan proposes that there are four primary stages of team development, each one requiring a contextual shift in leadership practice.

My research has revealed that developing high performing teams requires lead-ers to adopt flexibility in their leadership approaches. In practice, it requires a shift in leadership focus, objectives and behaviours to align with and support the evolu-tionary transitional processes of team development.

Stage 1: Dependency and Inclusion

All new teams regardless of their purpose or operational function begin their transi-tional journeys at the stage of dependency and inclusion. The primary focus for individual members in Stage 1 is personal safety. Roles, goals and structures are unclear and the team are dependent on the leader to be the focus of communication, providing direction and support. Wanting to be included and accepted, members communicate politely and tentatively, to avoid conflict. Individual members con-form and comply with the leader, to avoid realising their fears of rejection. A key characteristic of Stage 1 teams is that the leader tends to speak more than the team members. When the leader asks questions of the team, the norm is that they can be frequently met with silence.

Directive Leadership The primary objective for leading teams in Stage 1 is to cre-ate a safe environment. The leadership focus is orientated around encouraging members to contribute ideas and make suggestions by creating and facilitating pre-dictable patterns of engagement and interaction.

Directive Practices Require the leader to be assertive, confident and provide direc-tion, encouraging and facilitating dialogue focusing on core team values and pur-pose. The primary leadership focus is to support members to reduce projected fears of rejection by setting high-performance standards, providing positive feedback and guidance. Leaders act as the principal representative for the team, facilitating inter-actions with the rest of the organisation. They focus their efforts on reporting prog-ress, acquiring resources and fostering relationships with other teams and individuals, to manage expectations and mitigate the risks of unrealistic or exces-sive requirements.

Stage 2: Counter Dependency and Fight

In Stage 2, the team seeks to release itself from the dependency on the leader and conformity decreases. Facilitated by an increased sense of personal safety, members increase their levels of participation, feeling more confident to challenge the each other and the leader. Conflicts begin to emerge in the team as differences in views and perspectives are shared. Coalitions and cliques form as members begin to form relationships with colleagues that are more aligned to their own perspectives, opinions and world-views. The characteristics of Stage 2 teams are the impact of the felt sense and emotional qualities of discomfort, concern, frustration, irritation and even anger in some instances. Members dislike attending meetings because they find them physically and emotionally challenging, hard work and unproductive.

Consultative Leadership   The primary objective for leading teams in Stage 2 is to facilitate conflict resolution. Resolving conflicts encourages the development of building depth in relationships amongst team members through exploring and understanding differences.

Consultative Practices   Prompts the leader to see conflict as the key ingredient for establishing trust in relationships and a positive sign that the team is evolving into a new stage of development. In practice, the dynamics of Stage 2 teams challenge the leader to have self-confidence and not to take challenges to their leadership approach or position personally. The leadership focus is orientated on supporting the team to participate in shared activities of co-creating a unified purpose, defining values, goals and operational procedures. The leadership goal is to actively encourage and facilitate diversity of thought and differences in views, opinions and perspectives to establish common ground and build collective shared understanding.

Stage 3: Trust and Structure

As the team works with shared responsibilities and engages with continuing to resolve conflicts, commitment and cooperation increase. Communication becomes more flexible as individual differences are actively explored and tolerated. Members develop insights into understanding and knowing each other as they begin to build trusting relationships. Role clarity and consensus increase as team members work through differences and become more engaged and task-focused. New structures are created to increase the team's productivity. The characteristics of Stage 3 teams are members start to become more satisfied and accepting of each other. As they learn how to develop trust through building depth in relationships, they become more aligned with the team's agenda.

Participatory Leadership The primary objective of leading teams in Stage 3 is to return authority to the team. The focus for leaders is to facilitate active engagement in the leadership agenda, supporting the collective performance and outcomes of the team as a whole.

Participatory Practices Require the leader to empower the team to take account-ability for collective decision-making and the broader team agenda. The leadership focus is to share accountabilities and responsibilities amongst team members, utilis-ing sub-teams to accomplish tasks and achieve goals. The leader facilitates the design and implementation of changes in structures and approaches to enhance the team's operational functioning. Encouraging team members to act as ambassadors for the team, building partnerships and relationships with other teams and the broader organisation. Leaders actively promote and celebrate individual and team successes and achievements obtained from collaborative efforts.

Stage 4: Work and Productivity

As the team develops depth in trusting relationships, dialogue and sharing of infor-mation become frequent and fluid. The team as a whole expects itself to be success-ful, facilitating the creation of high-quality performance standards. Members align with each other's and the collective team's roles, goals, responsibilities and deliver-ables. Innovation, creativity, change and deviations from norms are actively encour-aged and supported. Sub-teams form, to lead new/different projects, define and design solutions to solve complex problems. Individuals actively seek and utilise feedback to enhance individual and team performance and productivity. Individual conflicts are frequent and brief, collectively supported by team conflict management strategies. The core characteristics of Stage 4 teams are a continuous positive focus on individual and team effectiveness and productivity. Team members go out of their way to support each other and take pride in promoting the collective efforts of their colleagues to impact the broader organisation.

Democratic Leadership The primary objectives for leading teams in Stage 4 are to harness the power of diversity of thought to encourage innovation. Leaders sup-port and facilitate the development of a team culture centred on continuous improve-ment, as a key contributory factor for high performance.

Democratic Practices The leader participates as an equal member of the team whilst monitoring the overall effectiveness of the team's functioning and activities. Encouraging individuals and the team to push boundaries and explore complexities and ambiguity so that they are utilised to develop new/different creative approaches. Leaders explore the broader internal and external environment for potential and the creation of new opportunities. The leadership focus is on how the team can make sustainable contributions to the core purpose and evolving strategies of the whole organisation (Table 6.1).

Table 6.1 Team leadership objectives and practices summary

	I Dependency and inclusion	II Counter dependency and fight	III Trust and structure	IV Work and productivity
Leadership Objectives	• Create a safe environment • Encourage members to contribute ideas and suggestions • Create predictable patterns of interaction	• Explore and understand differences • Facilitate conflict resolution • Build depth in relationships	• Return authority to the team and members • Facilitate engagement in leadership agenda • Enhance team performance	• Encourage innovation and creativity • Facilitate culture of continuous improvement • Harness the power in diversity of thought
Leadership Practices	Directive • Assertive and confident • Support members to feel safe • Positive encouragement and feedback • Facilitate open discussion of purpose, goals, values and roles • Set high performance standards • Provide guidance when required • Manage external environment	Consultative • Empower the team to participate in shared activities • Encourage diversity of thought • Facilitate shared understanding • Support individuals to resolve conflicts • Don't take attacks or challenges personally • Don't retaliate to challenges	Participatory • Empower the team to participate in collective decision-making • Involve members in the leadership agenda • Delegate leadership responsibilities to team members • Encourage members to act as ambassadors for the team • Promote and celebrate successes • Encourage the team to enhance performance and productivity	Democratic • Participate as an equal member of The team • Monitor team's performance and outputs • Explore internal and external environment to facilitate new opportunities

Flexibility of Leadership Styles

The implicit principle in what we have been exploring is that effectively leading teams through transitional stages of development requires leaders to develop flexibility in their leadership styles. In practice it requires leaders adapting the focus of their attention and aligning their practices with the evolving needs of the team that prompts drawing attention and awareness to a number of shifts in behavioural characteristics.

Spotting Transition Signals

There is no definitive timeline for how long teams remain in the different transitional stages. The leadership skill is to learn how to spot the key transitional signals that emerge in individual and collective team behaviours. The transitional signals for leaders to watch out for are:

Stage 1 Conflicts begin to emerge amongst team members and the team begins to challenge the leader.

Stage 2 Team members begin to resolve individual conflicts, develop depth in relationship and support each other.

Stage 3 The team begins to take ownership for their collective agenda, resolve challenges in processes, structures and relationships.

Through my own team leadership experiences, I have found that frequency is the primary clue. The more frequently the signals appear, the more evidence we have to know when to shift the focus of attention towards achieving the different leadership objectives. The process of focusing our intentions on the objectives creates and facilitates the context for adopting a different leadership style.

Knowing Leadership Preferences

One aspect that can hinder leaders acting on transition signals and flexing their styles is attachment to a preferred leadership approach. The unseen impact is that particularly in Stages 1 and 2, this can lock the team into a fixed stage of development. This is where leaders find themselves having to cope with low productivity, entrenched dysfunctional behaviours and the team becomes challenged to align with their core purpose and deliver productive outcomes.

The key contributor to this challenge is the misalignment of the leadership style with the developmental stage of the team. As we explored in Chap. 4, we tend to align our behaviour with aspects that we like and feel more comfortable with overlook, avoid or discount what we do not like. The impact is that this encourages repeated patterns of behaviour that act as blocks to a team's development. Case Study 6.1 illustrates an example of how these blocks can be manifested in practice.

Case Study 6.1 Stuck in Stage 1

Jenny, a clinical leader in a large mental hospital, reported that her team had been stuck in Stage 1 for seven years. As we benchmarked patterns in the team's functioning with Jenny's preferred leadership practices, we discovered that she had a preference for taking a directive leadership approach. Jenny's preferred approach was supported by the belief that it was her responsibility as a leader to keep things under control. As we discussed the reasons that underpinned Jenny's needs for control, she discovered that her behaviours were informed by fears of failure.

The primary concern for Jenny was that without directive input, the outcome for the team would be total chaos. Jenny disclosed that she would not be able to cope with a chaotic team as this would have a detrimental impact on her reputation and perceived leadership competence, by her line manager. What Jenny had not seen was that her preferred directive leadership practice had unintentionally created a group of fearful individuals. In practice what Jenny had done was unintentionally project her fear of failure on to her team. The outcome of Jenny's directive leadership approach was that her team were challenged to develop an integrated collective agenda because they could not share and value difference. The implicit implications were that valuing difference would require exploring, engaging and integrating new/different perspectives, which would initially result in conflict. The impact was that the team struggled to develop sustainable capabilities for navigating and embracing change. The team were perceived by other clinical functions, as being difficult to deal with, resistant to change and reluctant to engage in dialogue and contribute to innovation. The outcome was that the team were kept at arm's length by other parts of the organisation and engaged with on a transactional need to know basis.

Alignment with Core Capabilities

Insights into the preferred leadership practices can be found in knowing the primary and secondary core capabilities that we explored in Chap. 5. As we have previously highlighted, primary and secondary capabilities inform the what and how of different leadership practices. Here is how the core capabilities align with the different team leadership style preferences:

Production – Directive Leadership
Project – Consultative Leadership
Expert – Participatory Leadership
Relationship – Democratic Leadership

In the context of supporting the development of teams, a core resource for leaders to understand is the motivations, needs and drives that inform their core capabilities and how these create patterns in preferred leadership styles.

It is also particularly helpful to inquire into the edges of least preferred practices. Knowing the reasons that underpin the leadership style that we do not like, overlook and try to avoid is an essential self-insight practice when it comes to developing a flexible leadership approach. In this context, I have found that utilising Richo's principles of fear, attachment, control, entitlement (FACE) responses that we explored in Chap. 4 can be a helpful framework to support inquiry. Like in the above example of Jenny, where her primary need to want to control reinforced by her fear of incompetence, facilitated her attachment to taking a directive leadership approach.

Case Studies 6.2, 6.3, 6.4 and 6.5 illustrate examples of how inquiring into FACE experiences has been utilised to support the leaders to move out of the way of the transitional development of their teams.

Case Study 6.2 Transitioning from Directive to Consultative
Following the dismissal of a colleague, James inherited responsibilities for leading a global Executive Operations team. Acknowledging that the team had a reputation for being seen as arrogant and dysfunctional, James was aware that he was challenged, to build an effective team and to transform their reputation in the organisation. James was also aware that by taking the role, his strategic leadership capabilities were being watched by the Chief Executive and members of the board.

Over three months, James focused his attention on trying to create a safe environment. Directing his leadership activities on encouraging the team to design and build their strategic agenda by clarifying their purpose and defining performance standards. After three months of weekly meetings and several strategic away days, James began to experience what he perceived as decent amongst his team. Arguments and disagreements formed the foundation for the team's behaviours each time they met. As James tried to explore the reasoning behind the conflicts, he found himself in the firing line. He also noticed what he called "*cliques*" were beginning to form amongst team members who seemed to have their own agendas, that appeared to be misaligned to the team's strategic purpose.

James felt that his positive intentions and the efforts that he was putting into creating a supportive environment to build a high performing team, were not being seen or appreciated. He took the challenges to his leadership role personally and began to question if the team were out to get him fired, like his colleague.

As James reviewed his core capabilities, he discovered that his motivations, needs and drives were primary and secondary Production. Core needs to keep things structured and organised that facilitated the preference for taking a directive team leadership approach. He saw the core purpose of his role was to create structure and stability for his team and that conflict was a sign of "*descent into a black hole of unrecoverable dysfunction*" as he described it.

As James began to inquire into the construction of his perceptions, he disclosed that he was fearful of conflict. He was attached to the belief that harmony was the key to positive effective outcomes. Wanting to be seen by his team and superiors as an effective kind and caring person, James recognised that this was a primary need in all his relationships. James disclosed that he would go to great lengths to avoid upsetting colleagues, friends and his family. As we discussed the basis for his dislike of conflict, James realised it was a life-long pattern that had been formed in his childhood. Growing up in what he described as a dysfunctional family environment that consisted of *"daily aggressive arguments that frequently turned into physical violence"*.

As we discussed the alternative perspective that conflict is a natural transitional phase in the development of teams, James recognised that conflict was something that he had to learn to work with as opposed to avoid. James began his transitional development journey by seeking feedback from his family and friends. His objective was to draw awareness to the more subtle signals and aspects that informed his behaviour. James also shared the stages of team transition with his team and disclosed his conflict avoidance preferences. The outcomes were that his team suggested structuring a ten-minute feedback session into the end of the weekly meetings. James encouraged the team to comment on his behaviour while he was learning to develop new conflict resolution practices. Over two months the team engaged in a wide range of arguments and disagreements. James found the process challenging, and yet, by being open with his team, sharing his thoughts and feelings as and when they arose, he gained their support. Combined with the willingness to persevere and engage with the edges of his preferred responses, the team as a whole began to work through their challenges and develop depth in their relationships with each other.

Case Study 6.3 Transitioning from Consultative to Participatory

Ed, a technology programme manager, had been leading a European team responsible for delivering a range of software development projects. Ed felt that the team had made significant progress with working through their initial challenges of building a new technology strategy, developing new policies and working through their relationship challenges. Although at the same time Ed was becoming increasingly frustrated that individual members and the team as a whole seemed to be lacking in energy and motivation to drive their agendas. Regardless of topic, resolving difficulties and all decisions were fed back to Ed to resolve. Despite many conversations where Ed actively encouraged the team to take responsibility and actions, all roads kept leading to Ed

(continued)

Case Study 6.3 (continued)

to lead and drive the agenda. His boss had also informed Ed that he was likely to inherit additional responsibilities. Ed was concerned about how he was going to be able to accommodate extra responsibilities given that the team needed so much input of his time and resources.

As we explored and discussed Ed's frustrations, he concluded that the best way forward was to hold a meeting with one topic on the agenda that was to discuss the functioning of the team. Throughout a two-hour meeting, we uncovered a richer picture that brought a new perspective to Ed's perceptions.

Unbeknown to Ed he had earned himself the nickname of *"The All Knower"*. The team perceived that there was a difference between Ed's words and his behaviour. When team members went to Ed to gain input, he was quick to respond to help and support, at the same time, he also needed to understand the detail. Over time, Ed's need for detail facilitated a perception from team members that he wanted to know everything and be involved in all aspects of the functioning of the team. The team shared that they felt there was no point in empowering themselves to take actions because of the depth in his technical knowledge meant that Ed questioned everything. Appreciating and valuing his technical knowledge they were fearful that making mistakes and taking actions of their own accord would result in failures.

Ed was surprised and disappointed that his best intentions were not matching his or the teams desired outcomes. As Ed reflected on his team's feedback, he discovered that he had a fear of not-knowing, derived from the attachment to the belief that as a leader he should know the details otherwise he was not fully embracing his accountabilities. Ed acknowledged that his primary capabilities were Project and secondary Expert. He realised that his leadership frame-of-reference was formed on knowing the details, meant that he was in control. An unseen pattern that had been formed over managing the successful implementation of a wide range of complex technology projects throughout his career.

These insights encouraged Ed to make several adjustments to his leadership style and practices. His first transitional challenge was to learn to let go of his attachment to the need for detail and embrace that not-knowing was a typical trait for leaders at his level of seniority. As Ed reflected on how his not-knowing fears informed his behaviours, he recognised that he had to change his position in the team from being the all-knowing leader to embracing a participatory role. In practice, this meant transitioning the perceptions of his values, beliefs and perspectives on what it meant to be a successful leader while learning to develop new/different behaviours. Supported by his team, Ed learned how to redistribute his leadership responsibilities to team members and embrace a new practice of collective decision-making. The impact was that the team as a whole embarked on a development journey. They adjusted their approaches to problem-solving by bringing ideas and individual challenges to the team to share and explore options. Ed invited the team to hold up the mirror and challenge him when his detail and need to know traits made an appearance in team meetings.

As part of the journey, Ed discovered that he also had to let go and reframe one of his key motivations, in how he helped and supported individuals. Ed found himself in a push and pull tension of wanting to show support and at the same time not wanting to be or perceived as the all-knowing leader. Grappling with the practicalities of how to achieve his development objectives, Ed began encouraging individuals to explore potential options and solutions before asking him for help to provide the all-knowing answers and resolutions. Ed adopted a new response pattern, replacing *"this is how to resolve this"*, with *"what thoughts and ideas do you have about how you might resolve this?"* Over three months, Ed and his team redistributed their individual and collective accountabilities and responsibilities for the functioning and leadership of the team. The key success factors for Ed and his team were creating sub-teams to support innovation and learning how to utilise new approaches for collective problem-solving.

Case Study 6.4 Transitioning from Participatory to Democratic

Given the success of Ed's previous transition, this is how the rest of the journey evolved and the successful outcomes that he and his team achieved by transitioning his leadership style from a participatory to a democratic practice. As Ed's team built new operational structures and learned to own the collective team's agenda their productivity increased. As challenges arose, team members developed a new pattern of consulting each other and taking issues that could not be resolved to the team meetings to gain collective input and support.

Conflicts arose as team members openly shared their different world perspectives and compromising solutions were quickly found, as the team learned to value diversity of thought. Individual members took pride in supporting each other, reporting that they felt accountable for all team challenges and outputs regardless of their origins. When Ed's attachment to his expert inquiring mind made an appearance in team meetings, he was actively challenged. To the point that he was able to notice patterns in his thinking, adjust his responses and interrupt his behaviour when he felt that he was *"wanting to dive into the weeds"*. While not a straightforward task, Ed also challenged himself to let go of his need for detail and took on an expert advisory role. As the sub-teams developed, their own agendas, they took on many of Ed's lead-

(continued)

Case Study 6.4 (continued)

ership responsibilities within the broader organisation, deputising for him in technical and business forums.

Proficient in running their own agenda, Ed's team's innovations, stretched beyond how to improve their own performance to becoming a resource for embracing leading-edge technology solutions for the organisation. They earned themselves the reputation of being the *"go-to team"*. The more the team supported each other, their positive, capable resonance began to influence and support the broader technology agenda for the organisation. Ed's focus of attention transitioned into being the ambassador for his team. The outcome was that he created space within his agenda to build a new programme management function. The new function was comprised of three additional teams that were all at different transitional stages of development. By facing and working with the edges of his perceived leadership practice, Ed not only supported a successful transition of his team, he also transformed his career. The additional responsibilities that he took on earned him an Executive promotion that positively influenced the functioning of the technology division and the broader effectiveness of the organisation.

Case Study 6.5 Transitioning from Democratic to Directive
Kate was responsible for a financial project management office (PMO). As part of a restructuring programme, Kate inherited the responsibilities for leading a new team from the operations division. Wanting to create an integrated collective agenda, Kate invited the operations team to participate in the weekly financial team meetings. As Kate and her team had previously developed productive relationships with their operations colleagues, a factor that Kate had overlooked was that by bringing the two teams together, she was starting from scratch. Kate's newly combined team was in the Stage 1 phase of its development. While team members did know each other before the reorganisation, they had not had to participate in contributing to the same shared agenda. Kate found herself doing most of the talking in team meetings, and given that she had good relationships with all members, she could not understand why.

As Kate explored the different team leadership styles, she recognised that her core capabilities were primary Relationship and secondary Expert. Kate believed that her leadership responsibilities were to return authority to her new team to lead their own agenda. Kate reported that she enjoyed participating as an expert member of the team, sharing her knowledge and skills when required. The combined perspective of her perceptions of her leadership responsibilities facilitated a democratic leadership approach. Inquiring into the reasons that underpinned her preferences for this style, Kate discovered that it was derived from traumatic experiences of earlier stages of her career, what she described as being treated like a *"five-year-old"* by her line manager. She reported daily experiences of being told what to do and how to approach her work, directed not to question or challenge the views and behaviours of her manager. At the time Kate felt that she did not have a voice or any choices as to how she approached her work. Over two years of being on the receiving end of control biased behaviour Kate vowed to herself that if she became a team leader, she would never treat others the same way that she had been treated. As a consequence, she perceived any form of directive practices as being negative and went to great lengths to avoid them at all costs.

The first step for Kate was to reframe the context of her leadership responsibilities and practices. Kate learned to see and appreciate that setting clearly defined goals and high-performance standards was a critical factor in creating clarity and structure for her newly formed team. Not *that she was "controlling them and putting them into a box"*, which was how she had interpreted these practices based on her previous experiences. The focus of Kate's transitional development journey was to accept that her projected fears were derived from her own past experiences, that they were not the reality of her current situation. Using the transition cycle from Chap. 3 as a key resource, Kate recognised that this meant letting go of her attachment to the memories of her painful past experiences. In the process, Kate reframed her perspective of directive practices as being supportive leadership resources as opposed to negative, restrictive and debilitating. Kate shared the discoveries of her self-inquiry reflections with her team. She also asked for regular feedback so that she could learn to develop and embed new and different directive practices into her day-to-day activities.

Awareness of Transitional Shifts

What Kate's experience highlights is that in the normal functioning of organisations, teams are in the constant process of navigating transitions. Individual members join and leave; new business agendas are formed in responses to internal and external environments and market requirements. The fundamental principle is that even when teams do reach Stage 4 and are operating at high standards of performance, they are continuously susceptible to the impact of an impermanent landscape. The fundamental principles of impermanence make a call on leaders and their teams to have an awareness of the behaviours associated with the characteristics of the different transitional stages of team development. What may appear to be a relatively small change, like the addition of new responsibilities or the joining of a new member can initiate a substantial transitional shift for the team as a whole, while they learn to integrate new and different. Whilst the team may not take, as long to recover their engagement and productivity, it still requires leaders to be aware of and flex their practices, in alignment with the evolving transitional needs of the team.

Conflict-Handling Approaches

Whether we like it or not, conflict is a natural part of the process of developing depth in relationships. Working with conflict is a core competency for supporting teams to navigate their way through the different transitional stages. While facilitating conflict resolution is a critical factor for supporting a team at Stage 2 of its development journey, it does not end there as conflicts also emerge in Stages 3 and 4. Put simply, the ability to handle and facilitate conflict resolution is a core requirement for resourceful team transition leadership practices.

As with knowing and understanding preferences for team leadership styles, another resource for leaders is having insight into their relationship with conflict. In particular, paying attention to the type of styles that they may prefer to utilise when they find themselves having to deal with and lead others through a conflict resolution process. The primary reason is if there is a preference for a particular conflict-handling style and it is repeatedly overused, then it can have an impact on the team's developmental potential and performance.

Derived from Thomas and Kilmann's (1974) research, I find the labels from Levene's (1984) Launchpad diagnostic are the most straightforward. Levene proposes that there are five conflict-handling styles, what he terms as challenging, resolving, judicial, defusing and harmonious. This is how I have interpreted them and my experiences of the impact of any particular style if it is repeatedly overused.

Challenging Focuses on confronting the problem, utilising, arguments, logic, facts aggression, arm-twisting or even charm as approaches to dealing with conflicting situations. The purpose of adopting a challenging approach is to achieve a fast and economical solution to the problem. If the challenging style is overused, it can have a detrimental impact, where people on the receiving end report feeling 'beaten up and bullied'. The outcomes can lead to added complexities as members try to cope with their responses to continuous challenge that can make conflict situations more difficult to resolve.

Resolving This style focuses on getting to the cause of the conflict to sort it out. It involves actively encouraging both sides to put their cards on the table, to be open about their differences, feelings and perspectives in order to get to the root of the problem. The primary purpose of the resolving style is to reduce the conflict to find a long-term solution. The challenge with the overuse of this style is that people can feel pressured and exposed to reveal themselves, particularly for people who do not like to talk about their feelings. The outcomes can lead to reluctance and resistance to share perspectives, where the foundations of the problem can go underground, and root causes can be difficult to identify and work through. There is also a timeline factor, fully resolving conflicts can take time, which in some instances may be detrimental to achieving immediate or short-term operational requirements.

Judicial The focus of this style is to compromise and find the middle ground so that both sides can achieve something, where neither party is a clear winner. The purpose of this style is to introduce equality, reduce tension and the impact of emotional responses to establish common ground. The challenge with overuse of this style is that people feel as though they are continually being compromised. Where their individual needs are not seen, they are heard or appreciated. The outcomes can result in reluctance to give way that can show up as active resistance and stubbornness to explore alternative options.

Defusing This style seeks to avoid conflict or cool down the edge of its impact. Utilising subtle, tactful and diplomatic language and approaches to disperse tension, arguments and disagreements. The purpose of this style is to reduce the impact of short-lived emotional responses, and to avoid the long-term implications of *'making mountains out of molehills'*. The challenge with overuse of this style is that conflicts do not get fully resolved and *'molehills can become mountains'*.

Harmonious The focus of this style is to maintain and preserve harmony regardless of the causes or type of conflict. Seeing the other side in points of view and conceding, compromising and accommodating the needs and wishes of others. The purpose of this style is to maintain personal and professional reputation of being likeable, warm and open-hearted. It is driven from the perspective that sometimes, life is too short to fall out over differences. The challenge with overuse of this style is that it can impact the perception of leadership effectiveness. Leaders can earn themselves the reputation of being seen as a pushover, weak and easily manipulated by others.

What we have been highlighting is that one approach does not fit all conflict situations. That it is helpful to be able to draw on all of these styles, depending on the context. Based on my own leadership experiences, I have found that the defining factor is paying attention to our intentions and being mindful about what style to utilise to facilitate effective outcomes. Before making a conflict resolution intervention, I find that it can be helpful to pause, question and consider three key factors:

1. What is the desired outcome?
2. What is the style that is best fit for purpose to achieve the outcome (confront, collaborate, compromise, void or accommodate)?
3. What are the short and long-term implications of utilising this style?

When we handle conflict with purposeful intent, it provides informed choices in the outcomes that are achieved. In complex conflict dynamics, it is a regular occurrence that leaders find themselves making many interventions drawing on a range of different styles. I have found it helpful to view the different styles as a toolkit, flexing the use of the style that is best fit for purpose to meet intended outcomes.

As with leadership styles, it is useful to know the needs and motivations that inform our preferred conflict-handling approaches. Equally, the factors that inform our edges with what we tend to dislike or prefer to shy away from.

Summary
What we have been highlighting in this chapter is that developing high performing teams involves navigating, facilitating and supporting several different transitions both for leaders and for their teams. Developing teams requires an understanding of the different transitional stages of team development and spotting signals in individual and team behaviours, to know when new/different aspects are beginning to emerge. Leaders can support effective team transitions by developing flexibility in their leadership practices and conflict-handling styles. These approaches make a call on leaders to have insight into the preferences in their leadership practices, conflict-handling styles and how they are influenced by their primary and secondary core capabilities.

An Invitation for Self-Inquiry
To ground these concepts in applied practice, the invitation is to apply these concepts to explore your own team transition experiences. Here are a few questions to support your inquiry:

Your Team Transition Practice

Preferences

1. What is your preferred team leadership practice?
2. Why do you like this practice?
3. How do your primary and secondary core capabilities influence this?
4. How do your preferred practices support your team and leadership agenda?

Edges

1. What is your least preferred practice?
2. Why do you dislike this practice?
3. How do your edges inform and impact your leadership behaviours
4. What impact does this have on the development and productivity of your team?

Conflict-Handling Styles

1. Do you have preferred conflict-handling styles?
2. If so, why do you use these styles?
3. What styles do you tend to avoid, and why?
4. What impact does this have on your leadership practice?

Developing Your Team Transition Practice

1. How does the combination of your preferences and edges inform your team transition practice?
2. What do you want to interrupt, let go or develop to support your team transition practice?
3. What resources and support can you draw on to support your development journey?

References

Levene, M. 1984. *Launchpad diagnostic.* http://www.launchpadpsychometrics.com

Thomas, K. W., & Kilmann, R. H. (1974). *The Thomas-Kilmann conflict mode instrument.* Mountain View: CPP, Inc.

Tuckman, B. W. (1965). Developmental sequence in small groups. *Psychological Bulletin, 63*(6), 384–399.

Wheelan, S. A. (2005). *Creating effective teams. A guide for members and leaders.* Thousand Oaks: Sage Publications.

Chapter 7
Creating Supportive Environments

Introduction

The concept that we have been exploring so far is that there is no 'silver bullet' or 'one size fits all' when it comes to navigating the complexities and ambiguities of the transitional space. Depending on the business context and leadership agenda, how individuals approach and work with their transitional experiences varies. People can have the same experiences, and depending on their needs, motivations and capabilities, respond and behave in very different ways.

A key factor that supports individuals, teams and organisations to honour and work with the complexities of varied responses to transitions is to create supportive environments. Creating contexts of safety, mutuality and facilitating partnerships are key attributes that contribute to creating supportive environments in organisations. Supportive environments reduce the risks of complexity and ambiguity overwhelm generating contexts for facilitating creativity and innovation. These are key factors that enable organisations to use complexity and ambiguity to create competitive advantages in today's environments.

In this chapter we will be exploring the transition leadership practices that contribute to creating and sustaining supportive environments. We will begin by inquiring into the distribution of power and how it can be utilised to facilitate mutuality, followed by practical approaches for holding discomfort and concern.

Distribution of Power

There are many different perspectives on the utilisation of organisational structures, with flat being seen as a positive model and hierarchies now perceived in today's environment as being negative. What I have come to appreciate is that how organisations are structured is not the main challenge, particularly when it comes to

© Springer Nature Switzerland AG 2020
C. Hayes, *Transition Leadership*, https://doi.org/10.1007/978-3-030-42787-0_7

navigating the dynamics of transitions. We wouldn't have a school leaver taking up the position of CEO in a large global corporate organisation, because they would not be old enough to have acquired the necessary kills, knowledge and experience. In organisations structured hierarchies have a place, in supporting the development and utilisation of skills, knowledge and experience. The difference that makes the difference in practice is how leaders individually and collectively distribute and utilise the power of their responsibilities within their day-to-day activities.

A key question I encourage leaders to consider is how do they utilise the power of their leadership positions? Is power utilised to control individuals, teams, organisations and the business environment, or to facilitate mutuality to create shared understanding and build integrated partnerships?

It can be easy to say establish relationships and build partnerships and yet this can be difficult to put into practice without insights into the hidden dynamics of power. The distribution and utilisation of power tends to be overlooked, and/or taken for granted because it is a dynamic that influences every aspect of organisational functioning. This ranges from how an organisation approaches the market, the nature of their relationships with clients and the workforce, to how strategies and operational processes are implemented and utilised. Leaders and their workforces become like the 'fish that swim in the sea' they can't see the water because it's everywhere. Immersion in the dynamics of power permeates into the unconscious functioning of individuals, teams and organisations. Leaders become accustomed to the norms of how power is utilised and distributed because it is generally not something that they look for. Particularly, when it comes to the dynamics of how power is constructed and the impact that it has on operational functioning.

Developed for use in Transactional Analysis psychotherapy, Berne's (1964) ego-state concept offers a helpful framework to explore this territory. Also known as the PAC (Parent, Adult, Child) concept, the key notion being that we can knowingly or unknowing adopt these states of being in our relationships with others and ourselves. This is how it can be used to support inquiry into the complex territories of how leaders utilise and distribute power in their organisations (Illustration 7.1).

Parent Has two roles, nurturing and controlling. The nurturing parent utilises positional power to provide care and support for others. The controlling parent, also known as the critical parent, in an organisational leadership context assumes a position of power over others to dictate, manipulate or enforce requirements and rules to command compliance.

Adult When leaders adopt the role of adult they treat and engage others as equal human beings, regardless of age, role or position in the organisation.

Child Has two roles, free and adapted. The free child makes fun of others, playing games, acting without a care in the world regardless of the consequences. The adapted child can be represented in a number of ways; throwing tantrums, actively, or passively resisting authority and engagement. It can also show up as playing the role of victim, 'poor me', I am not seen, understood and/or respected. Depending on

Illustration 7.1 Parent, adult, child ego states. (Illustration by James Mellor)

how power is distributed throughout the organisation, the role of child can show up in both leadership and workforce behaviours.

Control = Risk Reduction

The principles behind the PAC concept are relatively straightforward; if people are treated like children they will behave like children. Responses can vary depending on the situation and personality of the individuals involved. For example, whilst facilitated by positive intent, if the leader repeatedly takes the role of the nurturing parent then this can impact the development and problem solving capabilities of their staff. People fall into a pattern of not learning how to think for themselves or act without guidance, referring to 'mummy or daddy' to solve all their problems. Equally if the leader takes the role of the controlling parent, they are likely to facilitate petulant responses, in the form of active or passive engagement. Whilst those who adopt the role of victims struggle to utilise their own resources, the outcomes can result in stunting the development of new skills and knowledge and how they progress their careers.

Control biased leadership practices have been honed over centuries and are still actively present in many organisations today. For example, initiating tight boundaries to manage behaviours, utilising hierarchical structures to broadcast information, encouraging top down decision-making, enforcing compliance of standards and rules. These are all examples of control biased leadership practices that have one primary purpose, to reduce risk. Intentionally or unintentionally, these practices create risk adverse cultures, because they focus attention on the performance, accountabilities and responsibilities of the individual. It is a practice that earned itself the nickname of the 'one throat to choke strategy'. The leadership principles behind using control-based strategies were if an individual's performance was not up to scratch then they could be replaced with a minimal impact on the functioning of their environments.

In today's organisations, control biased risk adverse environments stifle creativity, discourage innovation and impact the psychological safety of the workforce. Putting it simply, the overutilization of controlling parent approaches and their associated behaviours generate fear, evoking fight, freeze or flight responses. These responses in turn, facilitate the creating of toward, away (from) or against strategies that we explored in Chap. 4. The impact is a self-fulfilling cycle of fear based risk aversion responses that can facilitate political behavioural environments and cultures. The subliminal underlying message is that it's not safe to take risks, as mistakes are not tolerated and the consequential outcomes could be too detrimental.

Adult to Adult = Mutuality

Whilst being accountable for the performance and development of individuals and teams, it can be easy to overlook that organisations are comprised of adults. Yet, in reality if people are old enough to be employed then they are adults. Regardless of position or role, when employees are treated as adults, they have freedom of choice to be themselves. Individuals report feeling seen, valued and respected, for the parts that they play and contributions that they make to organisations. In short, adult-to-adult relationships facilitate mutually supportive environments.

The outcome of mutuality is that it creates the foundations for psychological safety that builds commitment and support on both sides. Leaders are able to support and challenge, inviting and receiving the same responses from their workforces, as we saw with the some of the team transition example case studies, in Chap. 6. When the leaders shared their frustrations and concerns, they were mutually challenged and supported to develop new skills and leadership approaches. The teams supported their leaders to see what they couldn't see and held up the mirror when unconscious patterns in behaviour made an appearance. This in turn created a supportive context for the leaders to understand the underlying causes that informed the preferences in their behaviours and to develop new team leadership practices.

Environments based on mutuality facilitate what I have come to term as 'move with strategies'. Move with strategies consist of returning authority to the workforce for innovation and decision-making and create collaborative approaches for complex problem solving. Leaders and their teams can leverage the power in diversity of thought, by drawing on a range of knowledge, skills and experiences to foster creativity and utilise potential from within their challenges. Not knowing is seen as a valuable commodity, where the less experienced workforce are seen as key assets for questioning and challenging the status quo. The input of new joiners to teams and organisations is actively encouraged and they play a key role in validating ideas and participating in the practical application of new/different strategies, policies and procedures.

Complexity and Ambiguity = Fear or Potential

How power is utilised can have a substantial impact on an organisation's capabilities for working with complexity and ambiguity. It can often be as stark as whether they see ambiguity and complexity as something to be fearful of and avoid at all costs or an opportunity to enhance productivity and create potential. As leaders consistently repeat patterns in thinking and behaviour, they create self-reinforcing cycles for themselves and the workforces.

The Fear Generating Cycle

The risk averse 'play it safe' context is the fear generating cycle in action, inhibiting our abilities for creating the new and different, from embracing and working with the associated complexities and ambiguities of transformation.

When faced with a complex ambiguous challenge, individuals seek safety within themselves. They focus their attention on trying to reduce complexity, as a strategy to support them to feel as though they are in control. In the process of attempting to reduce complexity and work with ambiguity they create and retain a perspective based on their own frame-of-reference to their current challenge. Utilising their self-comprised lens, individuals direct the focus on their attention and actions on their own agendas and what they feel they can control. As they attempt to work with and resolve their challenges, additional unseen factors begin to inform and influence their perspectives and approach that introduce additional aspects, complexities and eventually challenges to their personal agendas.

Trying to singlehandedly cope with added dimensions of complexity, individuals begin to experience symptoms of fear and anxiety. Fear and anxiety responses that prompts individuals to question their safety as their personal sense of being in control becomes challenged. In their attempts to obtain control individuals seek clarity, focusing their attention on what is known. The unintended consequences from individuals taking this approach, is that they develop a narrow fixed world-view. Trying to regain their sense of being in control, individuals lean into adopting transactional behaviours, interacting with others on a need to know basis. As more complex dimensions emerge, the intensity of ambiguity anxiety increases. The focuses of the individual agenda orientates around controlling themselves, the behaviours of others and their immediate environments. As multiple attempts to control different aspects do not match their desired outcomes, individuals seek safety from within themselves, often reducing and withdrawing from their relationships with others. Fuelled by a fear of failure, individuals begin to add unnecessary ambiguity and complexities to their challenge as their behaviours become derived from emotions and irrational responses. The more power they give to their responses to ambiguity anxiety, the more overwhelming their challenges become.

The Potential Enhancing Cycle

The potential enhancing cycle is informed by what I have come to term as the '*Move With*' strategy. Move with strategies are based on the foundations of mutuality that create systemic sustainable capabilities for navigating and working with complexity and ambiguity. The primary reason is that they facilitate psychological safety, because the focus of attention is based on accessing power through the collective. This is how the potential enhancing cycle works.

In collective environments support and challenge are facilitated through the formation of developing depth in relationships. When faced with a problem, people proactively seek to engage others, to evaluate and expand their frame-of-reference and understanding of their challenges. Facilitated through the process of dialogue, they create a context to explore associated complexities and utilise the views and perspectives of others to create alternative perspectives. The by-products of this process are that individuals create support and shared ownership of their problem. Individuals know that they are not alone and this facilitates felt sense qualities of safety and support to work with and through their challenges. The outcome of this collective approaches facilities an integrated world perspective, where the people involved adopt a systemic problem solving approach. The workforce can leverage the depth that they have built in their relationships to honour and work with complexity to utilise the potential within ambiguity, creating competitive advantages for their organisations (Fig. 7.1).

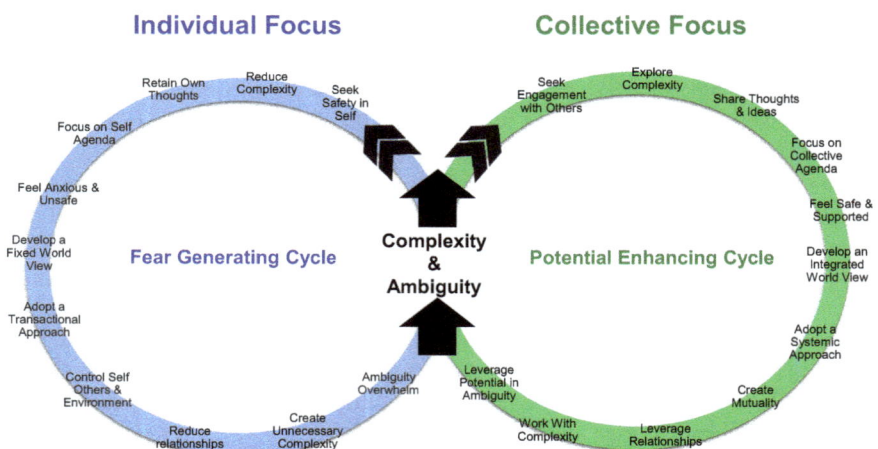

Fig. 7.1 Fear and potential generating cycles

Individual and Collective Power in Practice

I first became aware of the importance and practical impact of these self-reinforcing cycles in 2001. Since then I have observed these dynamics in many different organisations and operational functions across a wide range of different industries.

Case study 7.1 illustrates how these individual and collective cycles had a direct impact on the outcomes of revenue generation for a global sales division.

Case Study 7.1 Revenue Generating Approaches
The Executive team of a Global Financial sales division were grappling with an unknown aspect of trying to understand, why some teams generated between 20 and 30% higher revenue than others. On paper the logic didn't stack up, they were all operating in the same division and global market and yet there were distinct gaps in revenue generation. Working in partnership with 20 sales teams we conducted an inquiry into the practices that informed their operational functioning. Here is a summary of the key differentiating factors that we uncovered (Table 7.1).

Table 7.1 Practices of high and low revenue generating teams

	Individual low revenue	Collective high revenue
Market approaches	Work within market parameters, accept historical client needs and requirements as the norm	Utilises ambiguity, market structures and regulations to create new products and services
Primary strategies	Generates revenue through selling available products, providing a service to clients and responding to their needs	Generates revenue through partnerships with clients, product development specialists, support functions & regulators
Leadership practices	Manages client relationships. Advocates top down decisions. Individual responsibility for client accounts and sales targets	Celebrates individual/team successes. Challenges complacency and norms. Collective decision-making and joint ownership for client accounts
Team structure	Individual accountability and responsibility for client accounts and relationships	Collective accountabilities and responsibilities for the functioning of the team and client accounts
Operational processes	Communication, top down. Information shared through technology. Individual ownership for client accounts. Product knowledge achieved through training workshops	Communication, open and two-way. Information shared through dialogue. Collective ownership for client accounts. Product development achieved through client partnerships
Relationship approaches	Leaders hold different relationships with team members and others based on role and seniority. Leadership agenda separate from the team's agenda. Client relationships based on frequency and transactions	All team members, considered equal regardless of knowledge and experience. A focus on building trust and depth in relationships with clients, colleagues and industry regulators

(continued)

Case Study 7.1 (continued)

> At the time of conducting this inquiry we didn't know whom the high or low or revenue generators were. As we began to join up the patterns in the different practices, the impact of the utilisation of individual and collective power became clear. The operational context of the low revenue was based on containing and controlling risk. The operational context of the high revenue generating teams was based on mutuality and engagement to create potential from ambiguity and not-knowing.

Utilising Power

What case study 7.1 highlights is the way that leaders utilise and distribute power in their organisations can have a significant impact on employee engagement operational performance. The key factor is that when leaders focus on facilitating adult-to-adult relationships, they create psychological safety, fostering environments that create mutuality. This in turn means they can leverage collective power of their workforces to work with the inherent complexities and navigate ambiguities of continuously changing environments. Key enabling factors that support teams and organisations to transform challenges into potential.

Holding Discomfort and Concern

Supporting the transitional stages of team development, handling conflict and creating mutually supportive environments is reliant on another key leadership practice, of being able to hold discomfort and concern. A core practice that is essential when it comes to supporting others to navigate and work with the symptoms of ambiguity anxiety. As we have been revealing in other chapters, people can have the same experiences, and yet individuals will experience discomfort and concern for many different reasons. This makes a call on the leader to inquire into and work with the challenges of others, to create and facilitate a supportive environment. I have worked with many leaders over the years that have overlooked and dismissed this as a key practice. Primarily due to the fact that because they don't consider something to be challenging, they struggle to understand the causes of concern for others often forming the opinion that people are overreacting.

The underpinning reason for these differences in perspectives is that as complex individual human beings, our primary needs vary from each other, because they are influenced by traits that are informed by our personalities. The Humanist psychologist Heron (1992) provides a helpful perspective on primary needs. Heron proposes that the process through which we meet our needs is recursive. The meaning of recursive in this context is that we meet or not meet needs in the process of our relationship with others and our broader environment. Heron's view is that when our needs are being met, they have a fundamental impact on our sense-of-self in the world, contributing to our overall happiness and wellbeing. Utilising Heron's recursive principle in an organisational context, these are the core needs and associated characteristics that I have experienced can appear for people when they are being met (Fig. 7.2).

We grasp at getting our needs met and we don't take lightly to when they are not. When our needs are not being met, responses to our experiences form the main contributory foundations for discomfort, concern, fear and anxiety (Fig. 7.3).

Linking Sills's (2009) concept of the different territories of self from Chap. 4 with Heron's perspective, different needs become aspirations of the central-self depending on the context. For example, we may not expect to be cared for by everyone in professional context, yet when it comes to personal relationships, feeling as though we are being cared for by friends and our families can be a primary need for most people.

Building on Sills's concept of the needy-self, challenges to our inner felt sense of safety arise when our primary needs are not being met. A key factor that supports leaders to be able to hold discomfort and concern for others is knowing the core needs that inform their roles and how they influence behaviours. It is also useful to have insight into patterns in primary needs and transitory needs that may appear in particular circumstances and how they are similar and/or change in different situations.

We are all in continuous processes of negotiating the attainment of our primary needs in many different contexts. It is helpful to remind ourselves from time to time that it is not feasible to have our needs met, in all contexts by everybody all of the time. A useful approach is to explore contextual repeating patterns. If there are pat-

Fig. 7.2 Primary needs being met

To Choose		To be Chosen
Confined, powerless, constrained, restricted		Worthless, under-valued, overlooked
To Understand		To be Understood
Confused, lost, fearful, anxious, stupid, perplexed		Incompetent, undervalued, misunderstood, worthless
To See		To be Seen
Blind, vulnerable, uncertain, anxious		Overlooked, disregarded, worthless
To Care		To be Cared for
Ambivalent, apathetic, lifeless, frustrated, disconnected		Lonely, worthless, unloved, disregarded, neglected, abused

Fig. 7.3 Primary needs not being met

terns in certain situations, events or characteristics that evoke either positive or negative responses, then knowing how they inform our motivations, behaviours and relationships with others can provide us with choice in our responses.

To bring this concept to life, case study 7.2 reflects an example of the primary needs that have become the core of my central-self in the context of my work over the years.

Case Study 7.2 Cath's Primary Professional Needs

To Choose – having choice in how I approach my work is a core primary need. To the extent that now no choice = no engagement or work. In earlier stages of my career, where I found myself working for a line manager that utilised power in the form of a controlling parent, I felt constrained, restricted, disregarded and unappreciated. I felt as though I was seen and treated as an object as opposed to a human being. I dreaded going to work each day, and couldn't wait to find my next job to escape the experience of what felt like at the time of being trapped and imprisoned in my working environment.

To Appreciate – the organisation's strategy, agenda and the people I work with. I find being aligned with an organisation's strategic agenda inspiring, as it creates a context of purpose in where and how I can support them to make a difference for themselves. Equally, inspiring is being able to build partnerships and depth in relationship with my colleagues, where we can co-create outcomes that reach beyond our individual contributions. I find that if I cannot connect to the strategy or my colleagues the impact is that it becomes challenging to see how I can generate contributions that help them make a difference.

To Care – about the type of work I do. I chose my career path because I wanted to make a sustainable difference to the wellbeing of organisations. Seeing how my knowledge and skills can contribute to supporting individuals, teams and organisations make a difference for themselves fills me with hope and joy. If I don't enjoy my work then it drains my physical, emotional energy and significantly derails my motivation.

Transitory Needs – knowing what primary needs are at the core of my working practice, provides me with insight into what, how and who I engage with. Providing a useful context for supporting me to direct and navigate the path of where and how I conduct my day-to-day working activities. I have also found it helpful to understand what I term as transitory needs that are formed as a result of a particular context. For example, the needs of understanding and being understood have only appeared in the context of my academic studies. Where understanding to learn new/different concepts and being understood by others were at the heart of my primary needs because of the organisations that were judging my application of learning.

Creating Supportive Holding Environments

Whilst knowing the underpinning drivers for our challenges are founded on unmet needs another contributing factor for supporting others and ourselves to work with discomfort and concern is creating an environment of safety. Whilst the transition landscape may be challenging, I have found that leaders who can create a context of safety for their workforces, who find solutions to navigate their challenges, are the ones who successfully create and facilitate environments of potential.

The foundations for creating safe holding environments are based on establishing an empathic context. There are three core factors that contribute to building and holding an empathic context:

1. *Listening*
2. *Suspending judgement*
3. *Reserving interpretation*

Listening The qualities of listening can be frequently overlooked, because navigating the hustle and bustle of daily activities can often take centre stage. A question I frequently ask of leaders is do you listen to collate your thoughts and respond or are you truly hearing and understanding the other person and what they are saying? When we sense that we are truly being listened to we feel seen, recognised, understood, acknowledged and appreciated. This in turn facilitates a recursive loop that as listeners we are mutually appreciated in return.

Suspending Judgement One of the factors that can get in the way of our abilities to truly listen to others is how quick we are to make judgements. When we have a view or an opinion on something that may be different to others, it can often be challenging to refrain from judging others through our own frame-of-reference. We can't fully see, hear and honour the experiences of others if we are directing out thoughts and diverting our inner attention on making judgements.

Reserving Interpretation Another trait we as human beings can be partial to is interpreting and developing our own opinions and perspectives on what others are saying. The challenge with this is that we can often misinterpret key aspects of another's experience and get the wrong end of the stick. A question I find useful to ask myself whilst I am listening to others is how do I know what I think I know? Paraphrasing understanding and checking this out with the other person helps to avoid falling into the misinterpretation trap.

Energetic Resonance

Another aspect that is continuously present and yet often overlooked is energetic resonance. This relates to how we influence others through the energetic vibes that we project out into the world. For example, if we are happy, others know we are happy, because we may smile and look contented. Equally the same when we are unhappy, whether we openly share our inner experiences or not others sense that something is going on in our inner world lived experiences. Some of these signals are picked up through facial expressions and body language, there are also the aspects that we sense, which can be difficult to find tangible evidence for, put into words or describe. Whether we are consciously aware of it or not, we influence and are influenced by the subtle energies of our relationships with others. We can often intuitively sense when we are being judged and we know the difference when we are being supported or not.

Another key aspect to establishing an empathic context and holding environment is the qualities that we bring to what Sills's terms as our 'relational field'.

A practice that I learned whilst studying Core Process Psychotherapy, is how to bring resourceful qualities into the relational field that we co-create in our relationships with others. The Buddhist concept of the Brahma Viharas shines light into this territory. Sills proposes that the Brahma Viharas are comprised of four co-arising states, equanimity, compassion, loving-kindness and joy-in-resonance. Sills's view is that these states have the potential to emerge when we are fully present in the momentary experiences of the relationships. In applied terms the Brahma Viharas translate into:

Equanimity – Calmness and composure
Compassion – Sympathetic concern for the suffering or misfortunes of others
Loving-Kindness – Tenderness and consideration towards others
Joy-in-resonance – A feeling of great pleasure and happiness

I find that when we can fully utilise the resources of listening, suspending judgement and reserving interpretation, we naturally become fully present in the moment. We direct our attention and bring presence into our relational field that creates a context for the qualities of the Brahma Viharas to naturally emerge. A core resource that informs my own transition leadership practice is that I intentionally bring these qualities into the relational field to support people who are grappling with complex challenges.

Case study 7.3 provides an example of how I utilised the Brahma Viharas, to co-create a supportive empathic holding environment for a distressed HR professional.

Case Study 7.3 The Anguish of Andy

Andy, an HR recruitment specialist, described himself as feeling trapped and out of his depth. Off the back of the introduction of a new organisational operating model, his responsibilities had significantly increased. Andy had inherited a new strategic agenda for designing a talent development strategy and building a new function. He reported having no previous experience of strategy development and very little knowledge of organisational talent management. He was feeling pressurised by his fellow HR Executive colleagues to design and deliver something and didn't know where to start.

Andy's not-knowing and ambiguity anxieties were based on creating something that would by dysfunctional and fearful that the outcomes would cause him to be perceived as a failure. Andy was concerned that he would disappoint his boss, and produce something that would not be fit for purpose to support his colleagues or the organisation. He was concerned that the associated consequences would impact the development of his career and put his job at risk. Andy shared that his approach to trying to cope with his fears was that he had adopted a move away strategy. He avoided answering questions and queries from his colleagues and found a whole range of excuses to avoid attending executive meetings.

Andy looked stressed, he waved his hands franticly whilst sharing his story, the pupils of his eye were dilated and his speech was fast as though he couldn't get his words out quick enough. As I sat listening to Andy's story, and being present with his physical symptoms, I could sense the resonance of his emotional distress that felt like my body had been plugged into an electric socket. My arms were buzzing and I could feel my face tingling. My initial response was to ground the impact of Andy's stress related energy sitting upright and placing both feet on the floor (equanimity). Listening and suspending judgement, I found myself resonating with Andy's distress backed up with my own internal dialogue of *"I can only begin to imagine what this must feel like, to be in his shoes, bless him"* (compassion). The more compassion I felt for his experience, all I could think of was *"what can I do to help and*

(continued)

Case Study 7.3 (continued)

support him" (loving-kindness). As I allowed myself to sense, be with and support Andy's distressed state, I began to get a warm felt sense of potential in his challenge (joy-in-resonance).

As I summarised my understanding of Andy's challenge and empathised with the impact of his anxiety, the intensity of the felt sense of the potential in his challenged increased. I asked permission to share my thoughts and perspectives of the potential that could be created from his challenges and as I did, Andy appeared to calm and centre himself. He stopped waving his hands, sat calmly in his chair and leaned forward to listen. I shared the perspective that not-knowing and ambiguity whist challenging also create opportunities to learn new knowledge and skills. Andy reported that he was intrigued and responded with *"tell me more"*. The outcome was that we entered into a brainstorming dialogue about ideas and routes that Andy could take to gain the knowledge and skills that he felt he was lacking. At the end of our two-hour session, Andy reported that whilst he didn't feel his problems were resolved, he could see a pathway to begin to explore some different options.

One of those options was for Andy to own his concerns, to discuss them with his colleagues and ask for support. Specifically support to seek the input of a talent specialist, to assist with designing the new strategy and building a new team to implement it. He acknowledged that having become a recruitment expert not-knowing was at the heart of his deepest fears something that he hadn't faced for 20 years. He was embarrassed, and felt that as an expert senior leader he should know everything about the function that he was leading. I am pleased to share that over a period of three months, Andy sought support to develop the talent strategy and build a new function, that became a key resource to support the HR function, and open up a whole new pathway in his career.

Supporting and Holding Teams

We can also bring these practices of listening, suspending judgement, reserving interpretation and the qualities of the Brahma Viharas into our relationships with teams. I have found them particularly helpful for facilitating the development of teams whilst they are in the transitional of Stages 1 and 2 that we explored in Chap. 6.

Case study 7.4 provides an example of how I utilised these practices and qualities to support a challenged executive team.

Case Study 7.4 Executive Team Anxiety
Following the merger of six functions, a new executive team was formed to lead the creation and development of a new global financial division; four months into the merger, Steve, the leader of the division, sensed that all was not well. Steve reported that there seemed to be a lot of active and passive politics amongst team members. He was also aware that cliques were beginning to form and that there was a lot of what he termed as *"behind the scenes conversations"* taking place. The impact was that the team struggled to agree or reach consensus on what appeared to be the most mundane tasks. Steve was concerned that the team couldn't seem to *"get its act together"* and he was worried about the impact that this was starting to have on the implementation of their strategic agenda and the effectiveness of their division. I was invited to attend a weekly team meeting to provide an objective perspective of their functioning.

As I sat in the middle of a large oval boardroom table and the room began to fill up, I could sense that my body began to feel tight and stiff. By the time all ten members were seated and the door was closed, it felt as though a thick fog had formed above our heads; the well-known phrase 'you could cut the atmosphere with a knife' came to mind. Steve introduced me as an objective resource that had been invited to support the development of the team and their strategic agenda. Three members smiled, made eye contact and said thank you; two members folded their arms and stared at me; the rest of the team members were engrossed in their mobile phones.

As the two-hour meeting began, the feeling of the thick fog intensified. There seemed to be great disparity in the interactions and tones of people's voices as they spoke. Some individuals appeared tentative, stuttering and stumbling, others were confident and forceful, and a few kept quiet, focusing their attention on looking at the table and/or what appeared to be responding to emails on their mobile phones. Connecting the felt sense of intense fog with the physical behaviours of what appeared to represent as fight, freeze and flight responses, I became curious if what the fog represented was the collective energetic resonance of fear. My immediate response was to try to ground it (equanimity). Putting both feet on the floor, and drawing my own energy towards my toes, I sat back in my chair and continued to listen and watch what was happening in the room.

Twenty-five minutes into the meeting, the intensity of the felt sense qualities of the fog seemed to lift and what came with it was more evidence of move towards, away and against behaviours. I began to feel compassion for the members that wanted to positively move things forward, who appeared to be judged and blocked by their colleagues. As I listened to the differences in perspectives, I was also aware that the more challenging individuals were also

(continued)

Case Study 7.4 (continued)

experiencing their own responses to uncertainty. Sitting with both perspectives, my sense of compassion increased and I began to get a felt sense that people did care about the team's agenda; it was just represented in different ways. At that point I began to feel as though I was resonating with the events unfolding in the room and I felt a sense of wanting to support and care for the individuals and the team as a whole (loving-kindness). I began to feel a sense of potential (joy-in-resonance) sensing that what I was experiencing in practice, illustrated many signals of a team in Stage 2 of its transitional development journey.

For the following 30 minutes, I was aware that I was holding all four of the Brahma Viharas that began to fill me with excitement of the potential of working with the team to develop their agenda. I could feel the energy and excitement filling my whole body, as the fog seemed to dissipate. One team member seemed to sense my experience and kept making eye contact and eventually invited me to speak. Starting with the question, *"you have been sat there saying nothing for the last hour, and you look happy. I am not sure why you are smiling, but now you have seen us in action what's your view of what's going on here?"*

My initial response was to share the joy in my experience of the potential that I could sense. That prompted me to share the concept of the different transitional stages of team development, from Chap. 6. I invited the team to comment on where they thought they were on their journey. The content of the conversation shifted towards exploring the dynamics of counter dependency and fight that were present in the room at the time. As I shared my thoughts further dialogue and discussion emerged until we eventually ran out of time. We agreed to schedule another meeting to explore options for action and next steps.

We began the transition journey by incorporating the protocols of listening, suspending judgement and reserving interpretation as core team practices. This created a holding context to support the team to engage with conflict and work through their individual differences. At each team meeting I intentionally brought the Brahma Viharas qualities to bring supportive energetic resonance to the team as I took up the role of team development facilitator. Transitioning from Stage 2 to Stage 3 took the team two months, where each member and Steve the divisional leader were challenged and supported to navigate a wide range of personal transitional experiences. Whilst two months the team were in transition to Stage 3 were a bumpy ride, once the team eventually worked through their transitional challenges not only had they begun to develop depth in their relationships with each other, some member seemed to look more confident and at ease with themselves. Their workforce also noted the improvement in their effectiveness as a senior executive team.

Acceptance

One of our greatest challenges as human beings is that when we develop a perception or perspective, this perception or perspective forms and informs our frame-of-reference. Not just consciously for the situation where the perception or perspective is formed our frame-of-reference also sits in our unconsciousness, informing our view and experiences of the future. Perceptions become the filter that we use to see and hear that inform our experiences of others, the environment and ourselves. This filter informs our consciousness and becomes the lens that directs our focus of attention and becomes what we look for is what we see. Listening, suspending judgement, reserving interpretation and bringing supportive qualities to the relational field is founded on acceptance. Being fully present in the moment to hear, understand and support the experiences of others, by accepting and understanding just because our needs may be different to others, it does not mean that we can't be there to support them. At the same time, acceptance doesn't mean we take on or own the challenges of others. No matter how much care and compassion we give to others they can only meet us where they are, not where we are or where we may want them to be. Creating a supportive empathic environment requires patience, to be with and hold the experiences of others, whilst they find their own paths of working with their challenges.

Supporting and Holding the Self-Self Relationship

We can also apply the practices and qualities of creating a supportive holding environment to resource the nature of the relationship we have with ourselves. In times of my own experiences of discomfort and concern I find it can be helpful to explore three aspects of the situation:

Listening – drawing awareness to patterns in the Self-Self internal dialogue. Noting the content of the what and how the Self is engaging in conversation with itself.

Suspending Judgement – listening to what is being said without forming fixed perspectives of Self and/or the situation.

Reserving Interpretation – noticing the qualities of what is being perceived and looking for tangible evidence before forming a view or opinion of the Self. When perspectives do come into form, checking this out with others before taking action.

The Brahma Viharas can be useful resources to support challenging emotional responses, particularly experiences of complexity and ambiguity overwhelm. In times of challenge, this is how I utilise these qualities to resource myself.

Equanimity – sitting down, putting both feet on the floor and taking a few deep breaths, supports grounding and calming the energy generated by emotions.

Compassion – intentionally directing compassion to support the inner Self-Self experience, creates space and a safe context to explore the challenge.

Loving-Kindness – directing kindness inwards, interrupts and counter balances negative thought processes, bringing resources and appreciation to support the experience.

Joy-in-resonance – brings resources and perspectives to see light and new potential that can be generated from within the challenge.

A key aspect to bear in mind is that it can be challenging to hold these qualities for others if we can't hold them for ourselves. For example, for as long as I can remember I have always been my own greatest critic. It served me well whilst I was developing my career, pushing myself to learn more and developing practices for supporting others. Yet as time went on, I realised that the whole focus of my attention was on supporting others not on the relationship I had with myself. It wasn't until I began to study Core Process Psychotherapy did I realise that I needed to form a more resourceful relationship with myself. How could I be resourceful to support others if I did not support myself? In other words, supporting ourselves as transition leaders is a key resource for our abilities to be able to support others to work with the associated challenges of navigating the challenging territories that transitions evoke.

Summary
In this chapter what we have been unveiling is how leaders utilise and distribute power in their organisations can have a significant impact on employee engagement operational performance. When leaders focus on facilitating adult-to-adult relationships, they create psychological safety, fostering environments that create mutuality. That when combined with practices of listening, suspending judgement, reserving interpretation and the qualities that can be brought into the relational field, leaders can create supportive environments for their workforces and themselves. Aspects that reduce the risks of complexity and ambiguity overwhelm, generating supportive contexts that have the potential to facilitate effective performance, creativity and innovation.

An Invitation for Self-Inquiry
To ground these concepts in applied practice, the invitation is to explore your own relationships with power, how primary needs and approaches for creating supportive holding environments inform your transition leadership practice. Here are a few questions to support your inquiry:

Your Power Utilisation Practice
Leading Others
1. How do you utilise power in your own practice?
2. What impact does this have on your leadership agenda?
3. How does this impact the performance of the teams you lead and participate in?

Edges with Power Dynamics

1. How do you tend to respond if you are not treated mutually as an adult?
2. What impact does this have on your role and relationships with others?
3. What strategies and approaches can you adopt to facilitate adult-to-adult relationships when control dynamics make an appearance?

Your Primary Needs
Needs Being Met

1. What primary needs contribute to your happiness and wellbeing?
2. In what contexts does this occur?
3. What impact does this have on your thinking and behaviour?
4. How do these contribute to your leadership practice?

Needs Not Being Met

1. How do you tend to respond when your primary needs are not being met?
2. Are there any particular contexts or situations that trigger unmet needs?
3. How do these impact your leadership practice?

Alignment of Needs

1. How do your needs align/differ from those of your team/organisation?
2. How do these impact your leadership practice?

Creating Supportive Holding Environments

1. What practices do you currently utilise to create a supportive environment for others? (listening, suspending judgement, reserving interpretation)
2. What energetic qualities do you bring into your relationships with others? (equanimity, compassion, loving-kindness, joy-in-resonance)
3. How do these support your leadership practice?
4. What practices and qualities would you like to incorporate into your practice?
5. How can you utilise these to create a supportive holding environment for yourself?

Note 7.1
In this chapter we have explored the PAC framework in an organisational context. It can also be used to explore a range of complex dynamics, including the relationships we have with ourselves. Stewart and Joines (1987) have written a comprehensive text on this perspective.

References

Berne, E. (1964). *Games people play*. New York: Grove Press.

Heron, J. (1992). *Feeling and personhood. Psychology in another key*. London: Sage.

Sills, F. (2009). *Being and becoming* (pp. 262–263). Berkeley: North Atlantic Books.

Stewart, I., & Joines, V. (1987). *TA today. A new introduction to transactional analysis*. Lifespace
    Publishing. England & USA.

Chapter 8
Transition Practices

Introduction

Whether the focus is on continuous improvement to maintain a competitive advantage or to respond to change that is initiated by market trends or regulations, the only certainty in today's environment is uncertainty. There is, at the heart of the transition leadership practice, a paradoxical tension experienced when trying to work with the nature of uncertainty and at the same time whilst trying to hold the need for certainty for others. In the process of trying to work with the multifaceted dimensions that arise on the transitional journey, another dynamic that can unintentionally emerge is unnecessary complexity and ambiguity.

The impact of unnecessary complexity and ambiguity can be like pouring petrol on the fire of transition fear, anxiety and overwhelm responses. The outcome is that change agendas, programmes and projects can become trapped in recursive self-fulfilling loops, which erect veils inhibiting the abilities for honouring complexities and navigating the core ambiguities present in all change agendas.

This chapter focuses on unveiling the factors that contribute to unnecessary complexity and ambiguity. It explores key business risk mitigation practices and approaches that support individuals, teams and organisations to navigate the different territories of the transitional space.

Clarifying Purpose

When leaders lean into and act out the symptoms of transition blindness a (oversimplification, haste, impatience) a concept that we explored in Chap. 2, one of the first leadership practices to go out the window is spending time and effort to clarify purpose. A frequent response I receive from leaders when I ask about purpose is, *"everything keeps changing, and so what is the point in wasting time and effort on*

© Springer Nature Switzerland AG 2020
C. Hayes, *Transition Leadership*, https://doi.org/10.1007/978-3-030-42787-0_8

this". Based on my own experiences, once purposes have been established they only tend to need adjusting under conditions of major structural redesign and or transformations such as merger and acquisitions of business functions and organisations. They do not require amending that frequently if they are aligned with the core functioning of the organisation. Leaders create significant challenges for their organisations when they do not invest time and energy in creating and clarifying the purpose of their organisations, transformation programmes and projects.

A clearly defined purpose frames the context and articulates the reasons why something exists. When we know why something exists, it facilitates a meaningful heart and mind connection to it. The primary reason is that it supports the fulfilment of our innate human desires to contribute to something bigger than ourselves. Having clearly defined purposes in organisations create meaningful contexts that support individuals, teams, functions, divisions and organisations to understand the contributions that they can make.

Purpose also creates the framework that informs the focus for day-to-day activities. Clearly defined purposes support leaders to return authority to individuals, teams, functions, divisions and the organisation as a whole. Knowing purpose frames the context for focus, daily activities and practical execution of the broader agenda, supporting the processes of decision-making, future planning and innovation. Here are a few key strategic questions that having a clearly defined purpose can help to answer:

1. If something is not in alignment with the core purpose, then why is it being done?
2. Is what we are planning to do in line with our core purpose?
3. What new products and services can we create that aligns with our purpose?

The challenge with not clarifying purpose is that it can generate ambiguity in multiple contexts throughout and organisation. Figure 8.1 illustrates what happens when leaders overlook the importance of investing time in creating and encouraging the development of purpose statements in their organisations.

Unfortunately, I have witnessed the presence of unnecessary ambiguity on many occasions, in organisations across a wide range of industries. It is challenging for individuals to connect and feel like they can make a valuable contribution to their teams when they are unsure of the activities and the focus of their own roles. The same applies to how teams contribute to the agendas of their functions, divisions and the organisation as a whole. When individuals align the focus of their activities and contributions with the broader organisational context, the combined outcome contributes to creating an environment of integration and psychological connectivity. Psychological connectivity contributes to individual and collective motivation and engagement. When the practice of creating purpose in multiple contexts is embedded into the leadership tool kit, organisations find that the origins of ambiguity are associated with the external environment. Internal complexities can be honoured, and ambiguities can be worked with, through the power derived from collective, integrated agendas.

Focus & Activity Context

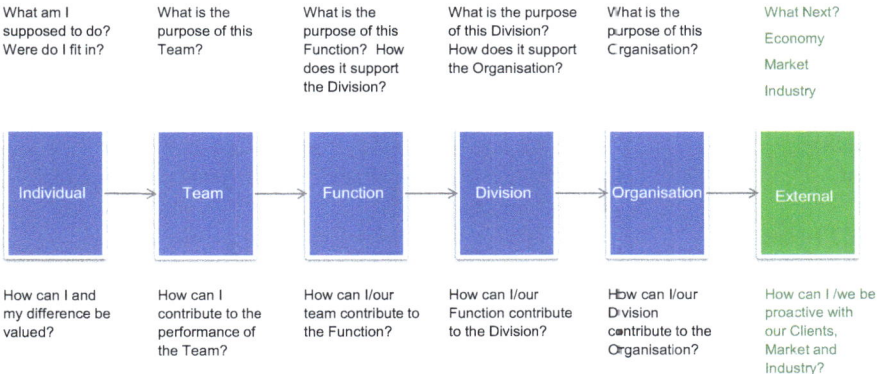

Fig. 8.1 Unnecessary ambiguity in organisations

When it comes to leading change and transformation programmes, clarifying the purpose of change is an essential task. How can we expect people to engage with the associated challenges of a transition process if they do not know why the change is happening? Not-knowing the reason for why something exists or is happening deepens the psychological attachment to what is known. If the fundamental question of why a change process is taking place cannot be answered, it raises further questions, triggering a whole range of defensive and ambiguity anxiety-related responses. People begin to question the consequences of the unknown and the potential impact that this may have on their day-to-day activities, working practices and the operational functioning of their environments. The outcome is the preference to lean into the safety of what is known to avoid the uncertainties of stepping into what is unknown.

Developing Purpose Statements

While supporting leaders and their teams to create purpose statements, I find that it is useful to work with three core principles:

1. *Keep it short* – one sentence
2. *Clear language* – choose words that are applicable to the whole organisation
3. *Jargon-free* – use terms that anyone outside the organisation can understand

Here are a few organisational examples from a range of different industries that align with these principles:

Organisation

Google   *"Organize the world's information and make it universally
                        accessible and useful"*
Walt Disney   *"To make people happy"*
Kellogg   *"Nourishing families so they can flourish and thrive"*
IAG   *"Help people manage risk and recover from the hardship
                        of unexpected loss"*
SETI Institute   *"Explore, understand, and explain the origin, nature,
                        prevalence and distribution of life in the universe"*
ING   *"Empowering people to stay a step ahead in life
                        and in business"*
Merck   *"Preserve and improve human life"*
Hewlett-Packard   *"Make technical contributions for the advancement
                        and welfare of humanity"*

I do not know all the products or services that these organisations provide, yet when
I read their purpose statements, the context that they operate within and their focused
intent is clear. As a potential client of these organisations, I have a sense of what
they are all about. That is the core purpose of a purpose statement. Here are a few
more examples:

Function and Division

Mental Health   Providing care and support to the mental wellbeing
                        of our community
Training   Building a first-class workforce by enhancing the skills,
                        knowledge and capabilities of our people
Finance Reporting   Produce financial reports so our clients can receive
                        timely quality investment information

Individual

Trainer   Designing and delivering development programmes
                        in line with the needs of our business and people
Sales Executive   Building partnerships with clients to provide solutions
                        to enhance the performance of our businesses
Project Manager   Engages colleagues and clients to create an
                        environment for facilitating change, to a defined
                        outcome, budget and timeframe

Co-creating Purpose Statements

I use the term co-creating because developing powerful purpose statements requires collective input and diversity of thought to create and validate their impact. This is the process that I utilise while supporting teams to develop purpose statements:

1. *Prepare* – schedule a dedicated team meeting, a minimum of two hours.
2. *Brainstorm* – framed by the question, what words represent, what we do, and why we are here? Each team member creates a list of six keywords that for them align and relate to the core purpose of the team, project, programme, division and so on. This activity can take place before or at the beginning of the meeting.
3. *Review* – individual members share their words, and the team chooses the words that resonate and align with their views and perspectives. I find it is helpful to use sticky notes, flipcharts and a whiteboard for this process.
4. *Draft* – framed by the question, what is the purpose of our organisation/division/function/team/project? Using the key selected words, the team creates a preliminary first draft of the statement.
5. *Evaluate* – share the first draft with a broad audience (colleagues from other teams, functions, internal and external stakeholders).
6. *Redraft* – incorporate the feedback into the preliminary version and create a second draft.
7. *Validate* – with colleagues and stakeholders. Where possible, at this stage, it is resourceful to seek feedback from people who are objective or independent from the team.
8. *Create* – incorporate feedback and create the final version.

The qualities of listening, suspending judgement and reserving interpretation that we explored in Chap. 7 are all resourceful practices to support this process. Although a word of warning, creating and developing purpose statements requires an investment in time and patience, it does not happen overnight. Depending on the different complexities of the task, I have known some teams to spend up to four full days creating the preliminary first draft and two weeks to complete the whole process. I have also found that if teams skip steps or try to rush this process, they can end up with something that is not fit for purpose that defeats the objective of the whole exercise.

A key factor for knowing when to stop is to watch out for repeating patterns in topics and language. If different words are used to describe the same context then it can be helpful to focus on understanding if there are any differences in their underlying meaning. For example, what are the differences between the words building and developing? If in practice they have the same meaning then it comes down to making a call that can often result in calling a vote for preference.

Co-creating Additional Benefits

Framing the context of why and providing clarity, developing purpose statements has several additional benefits. Building on the practices of developing teams, from Chap. 6, when conducted with teams at Stage 1, co-creating purpose statements can be utilised as a unifying team activity. Creating a team purpose is also a useful process for supporting transitional journeys into Stage 2 and framing the focus for activities as the team transitions into Stage 3; this is how it works in practice.

As the team engage in creating a single unifying purpose statement, they enter into a process of co-creating a context for exploring different world-views and perspectives. This process facilitates collective learning for working with and valuing the difference in views, opinions and perspectives. The outcome is that the team enters into a process of acceptance. Valuing difference and acceptance are the key contributory factors for honouring and working with complexity. As the team learn to work with and resolve the conflicts that arise from their differences, developing trust and depth in their relationships, they co-create a context of support and commitment. The team's purpose becomes the central organising framework for day-to-day activities and the contribution that they make to the broader organisation.

Aligning Individual Contributions

A useful exercise for aligning individual contributions with the team's agenda is to create role purpose statements. Once the team purpose has been created, the team can then co-create the same for individual members. The same principles apply. With regards to the approach, I find that it is helpful for individuals to begin by creating the first draft and then to share and gain support from their colleagues to complete the final version.

Systemic Integration

My experience of high performing and effective organisations is that they are reliant on the integration of systemic relationships. Different teams, departments and divisions have a purpose in contributing to the functioning of the organisation as a whole. If they don't, then it raises the questions of what purpose do they serve and why are they there? Another factor that contributes to unnecessary complexity and ambiguity is a process that I have come to term as splitting.

Splitting relates to how individuals, teams, projects, programmes, departments and divisions operate as single independent entities. A term often used to describe this is silo mentality. Unfortunately, when it comes to the process of navigating transitions, splitting facilitates a narrow focus, which means that the power gained from systemic functioning and mutuality-based environments cannot be fully utilised. Change functions and transformation agendas are now given labels, like people, process, technology, compliance, operations and finance, to name just a few. We only have to look at how many different types of change roles are advertised on LinkedIn to see how prominent splitting has become in today's organisations.

Integrated systems are comprised of multiple processes of co-evolving interactions where all aspects are reliant on each other to create effective operational functioning. For example, sales are reliant on the provision of quality products and efficient distribution infrastructures that will all require the input of technology. Also, let us not overlook the fundamental fact that people are at the heart of the functioning of organisations. Artificial Intelligence has not fully replaced people in executing effective functions and services in organisations quite yet.

Combined with the symptoms of transition blindness, the outcome is more often than not tunnel vision. The impact of tunnel vision when navigating the complexities of the transitional space is factors that fall outside of a narrow focused perspective will often be overlooked. An aspect that I frequently experience in organisations is that is not until transformation projects are well underway, that the practical implications of splitting fall into awareness. The outcomes can range from having to retrace steps, leading to increases in timelines and budgets to complete project or programme failure.

Methodology Mind-Set

A key contributor to splitting in organisations is the methodology mind-set. Programme and project managers acquire these different mind-sets through the focused application of project management approaches and methodologies. Waterfall, Lean, Prince2, Agile, Scrum, Kanban, Crystal, PRiSM, Critical Path are just a few of the approaches and methods that are used in organisations today. While these methods and approaches are useful frameworks, they can also become the foundations for unconscious attachments to fixed approaches for execution. What often goes unnoticed is that these attachments create a focused lens and pathway, where people become reliant on the methodological approach, to deliver their intended outcomes. While teaching several project management methods and approaches in earlier stages of my career, over the last 25 years, I have formed the philosophy that no single methodology fits all purposes. The most effective approach is to choose the method that is best aligned with the purpose and needs of the transformation process. I have found that it is more resourceful to have access to a tool kit of different methods that can be drawn on and utilised to inform design and support effective execution.

Understanding Operational Functioning

An approach to mitigating the potential risks of methodology mind-sets is to gain insight into the broader context and operational functioning that informs and influences the programme of work or project. The purpose of understanding operational functioning is to gain insight into what is informing the nature of the transitional space before stepping into it. Knowing operational functioning can be utilised to draw awareness to factors that can often sit outside or on the periphery of the initial programme of work or project plan. Understanding the dynamics of operational functioning supports programme and project managers to incorporate an integrated perspective to inform their transformation strategies and execution plans. It is a useful inquiry practice that provides insights that can be utilised alongside preferred methodologies. Conducting inquiries into operational functioning creates an integrated lens for framing the transitional context. A resourceful context that can be utilised support the design and approach for the initial start-up phases, and during the execution of transformation projects.

A factor, I see in many transformation projects is that attention is directed on the future, without understanding how what is happening in the now may inform effective execution and delivery, the transformation programme or project cannot fully leverage and build on what is currently working. Or alternatively operational oversight can unintentionally break aspects that are of benefit to the programme of work and the organisation as a whole. An approach I apply to all transformation programmes is to invest time in understanding the existing context. Before creating a transition execution plan, it is helpful to gain as much information as possible about the current operational functioning that surrounds and informs the intended change process.

While the key question is 'how is this environment currently functioning?' I find it particularly useful to inquire into several different aspects:

Objectives – what is the purpose of the change? Why is it important? How does this contribute overall to the organisation's purpose and future strategy?

Impact – what is currently working/not working in the existing environment? Who will this change impact and in what way?

Focus – what is the scope of this change process? Where do the boundaries of change begin and end? What factors will we need to take into consideration?

People – what are the primary and secondary core capabilities involved in this change? What are the implications on current/future capabilities skills, knowledge, skills and behaviours for leaders and the workforce?

Technical – what are the implications for existing structures, processes, systems, technology and working practices? What will need to be adapted or implemented?

Ambiguity – what is known and unknown? Are there any complex, ambiguous or divergent aspects involved?

Culture – How will this change impact the existing culture? What are the potential implications for the day-to-day operational environment?

Stakeholders – Who are the key stakeholders?
Risks – What risks are associated with this change? What will we need to take into
   consideration?

To bring the value of the impact of this exercise to life, case study 8.1 illustrates
an example of what an inquiry into gaining insight into operational functioning
reveals.

Case Study 8.1 A New Client Relationship Management Approach
Following a global reorganisation, the senior executive team of a newly
formed retail sales division identified that they had a systemic challenge.
While reviewing their annual revenue statistics, they found that they had done
many different transactions with the same organisations Regionally and glob-
ally, the executives found different teams had relationships with the same client organisations, and they were all operating independently from each other.
The concern was that they were missing out on the potential of new and repeat
business because they did not know who had the same or different client relationships and connections. The executives were also worried about reputa-
tional risk; by not being joined up, how this might impact ongoing client
relationships; and their strategy for being perceived as partners and long-term
solution providers.

The executive team were aware that some departments and teams had
developed their own Client Relationship Management (CRM) processes and
systems. The executive team's initial strategy was to implement a new central
global technology CRM system that could be utilised by all teams and departments. Four months after implementation, realities were not matching aspirations. The executive team found significant discrepancies with the quality of
the data and some departments and teams had not used the system at all.
Table 8.1 is a summary of the findings from the initial review of the operational functioning of the different CRM approaches across the retail sales
division.

This high-level view revealed a whole raft of complex dynamics that emanated from the global reorganisation process. Discussing this summary with
the executive team, they realised that the origins of their challenge were
related to forming their new division. This inquiry into the operational functioning of the division revealed that little had been done to create new global
integrated working practices. Client relationship management was not the
only aspect of their division that required systemic alignment.

The executive team acknowledged that they had been unrealistic in hoping
that a technology solution alone would solve all their problems. They also
acknowledged that they by adopting a narrow view, they had underestimated

Case Study 8.1 (continued)

Table 8.1 Operational functioning current state summary

CRM Programme Current State	
Objectives	Purpose – Unite our sales force and generate collective client intelligence
	Why – To create opportunities for increasing revenue and enhance client relationships
	Strategy – To generate revenue through building trusting partnerships
Impact	Working – Some global departments and teams have an integrated approach
	Not Working – More departments are not using the CRM process than those that are
	Who – This programme will impact the whole sales division of 2500 people
Focus	Scope – A global transformation process involving all retail departments
	Boundaries – Retail only
	Key Factors – Develop a robust practice that can be shared with other client-facing divisions
People	Core Capabilities – A mixture of Expert-Relationship and Expert-Expert
	Implications – Leaders and teams will be required to develop new skills and practices
Technical	Processes – New global reporting and information-sharing policies, protocols, practices
	CRM System – May need adjustments to align with new processes
Ambiguity	Known – Some leaders and teams will be attached to their existing practices
	Unknowns – How resistance may impact the workforce and client relationships
Culture	This programme intends to create a new unifying integrated operational culture
Stakeholders	Exec leadership team. Department & team leaders. Business Partners IT, HR, Compliance
Risks	Splitting – Coalitions may form amongst teams who do not want to change their practices
	Flight – Some people may leave the organisation
	Relationships – Resistance may impact or influence key internal or external client relationships
	Outcomes – Nothing will change because of the attachment to existing practices

the complexities that were informing their desired outcomes. The focus of our programme of work evolved into supporting the development of an integrated operational infrastructure, where building a global CRM approach would be utilised as the facilitator of the broader divisional integration process.

Adjusting the context of our programme of work raised more questions, about the activities and the approaches that we could undertake. The next step was to build a transition strategy.

Transition Strategies

The purpose of a transition strategy is to gain insight into the size of the gap between the current state and future desired outcomes. Transition strategies are informative resources at the outset of a transformation programme or project. The transition cycle that we explored in Chap. 3 is a useful resource for prompting key questions to inform the formation of transition strategies:

Phase 1 Shifting – what will be required to be dismantled and deconstructed?
Gateway 1 – what norms and familiar ways of working will be interrupted?
Phase 2 Ending – what will be required to disintegrate and dissolve?
Gateway 2 – what known practices will be required to let go of?
Phase 3 Emerging – what will need to be reformed and reconstructed?
Gateway 3 – what capabilities and operational practices will be required?
Phase 4 Forming – what new approaches and practices will be required to be developed and implemented?

Case study 8.2 illustrates the information that was gained at the outset of the CRM programme.

Case Study 8.2 CRM Programme Transitional Insights (Table 8.2)

Table 8.2 CRM insights

Phase 1 Shifting	What will be required to be dismantled and deconstructed?
	"The diverse CRM practices policies, processes, procedures of the departments & teams within the Retail Sales Division"
Gateway 1	What norms and familiar ways of working will be interrupted?
	"The preferred CRM practices of some individuals, teams & departments"
Phase 2 Ending	What will people be required to disintegrate and dissolve?
	"Established practices for sharing client information within their separate teams & departments"
Gateway 2	What known practices will people be required to let go of?
	"Individual, team & department autonomy of client relationships & transactions"
Phase 3 Emerging	What will need to be reformed and reconstructed?
	"A new integrated global divisional CRM operating model"
Gateway 3	What capabilities and operational practices will be required?
	"Collective ownership, accountability & responsibility for existing client relationships to inform the creation of new integrated partnerships"
Phase 4	What new approaches and practices will be required to be developed and implemented?
	"Collective ownership, accountability & responsibility for existing client relationships to inform the creation of new integrated partnerships"

Utilising Complexity

Sometimes these questions can be easily answered, and the information obtained can contribute to building a plan for execution. In more complex programmes if these questions cannot be answered, then it is also a great insight, primarily because it highlights the requirement to honour the complexities and find approaches for working with unknown dimensions. For example, in the case of the CRM programme, the unknowns were specifics about the diversity in different CRM practices. At the outset, we were aware that there were some effective CRM practices that we may want to leverage and replicate in the new divisional operating model. We also did not have enough specific information about the differences and size of the gap between what was and was not working in practice. These unknowns gave us valuable insight into designing our starting point. Once we have a sense of the context, how something is functioning and the factors that are informing it, then we have a choice in what approaches we can take.

Transition Leadership Approaches

Another common unseen aspect is the impact of how the programme/project is approached. The philosophy we have been working with so far is that we cannot manage change it is about learning to work with it, although we can manage projects.

The approach that we take to managing programmes and projects is a fundamental aspect that requires careful consideration. While leaders, teams and organisations may have a positive intent, the way they approach a change agenda will have a significant impact on the effectiveness of the transition and implementation processes; as we saw in the example of the Financial Change Function case study 4.2 in Chap. 4, who took a controlling parent governance approach in their attempts to deliver successful outcomes. The critical factor to be aware of is paying attention to our intentions and actions that inform our approaches.

Holding a Neutral Position

My preferred approach, while leading any kind of transformation process, is to walk the middle path. In practice, this means taking and holding a neutral position of supporting the strategy, wellbeing of the programme of work and organisation as a whole. Quite often, stakeholders and leaders can unknowingly or unintentionally influence and are the root causes of their own challenges, and this is where holding a middle ground context is helpful.

In practice walking the middle path requires listening, suspending judgement, reserving interpretation that we explored in Chap. 7. It also means being the ambassador of the transformation process. In practice it requires being prepared to hold up the mirror as and when needed to support aspects that are in line with the purpose of the transformation process and challenging factors that do not. The focused intent is being open to the diversity of different views and perspectives of others. Plus being mindful of the positional power of key stakeholders and trying not to take sides regardless of their status or position in the organisation. Just because something might be perceived as being good or bad by a key stakeholder, that does not necessarily mean in practice; it is the case. Taking sides does not support effective transitions; in fact, it can hinder it. Primarily because, if fear-driven passive or active resistance is present, we as programme/project managers run the risk of being seen as representatives of the bad and what is not wanted.

Being representatives of the change process and holding a neutral position supports us as transition leaders to focus on the potential that can be generated from the transformation process. This means that we can be seen as supportive resources to the workforce, the programme of work and ultimately the organisation.

Another aspect to be mindful of is how we take up the ambassador role, being careful not to become too personally attached to the programme/project. To ensure that the role of an ambassador is not used to force outcomes, or that we put ourselves in the position of being seen as driving our own personal agenda. Our role as ambassadors is to support the complexities of the transition process to achieve effective outcomes for the organisation as a whole. Being an ambassador means putting the organisation's agenda at the forefront of our frame-of-reference and drawing awareness to how we walk the middle path while holding and representing the context and purpose of change.

Core Capability Alignment

Outcomes from core capability mapping exercises, the principles that we explored in Chap. 5 can provide valuable resources for designing transition strategies. Understanding the primary and secondary core capabilities that are influencing and informing the change process provides informed choice in the types of approaches that can be taken. The primary purpose is to reduce the risks of generating unnecessary complexity and ambiguity by being aware of the primary needs that underpin the existing environment. Also, knowing the potential edges that are likely to appear if the key needs of the people who will be impacted by the transformation are not taken into consideration. Here are some factors to consider that are useful to inform planning and designing approaches at the outset and during the execution phases of transitional processes.

Production The core needs for production are seeing and following a structured process. Resourceful transition approaches in production environments are communicating the transition strategy at the outset and providing an overview of what the pathway ahead may look like. Shared with the caveat that what is planned may change over time in line with unknown aspects that may emerge along the journey. In environments, where production capabilities are prominent, it helps to provide frequent updates of progress, paying particular attention as to how these may impact the intended course of direction. The intent is to be as transparent as possible about what is known to mitigate any associated risks of projected fears of not-knowing what will happen next.

Project Having a defined purpose and insight into targeted outcomes are core needs for project capabilities. Project capabilities like to see the bigger picture at the outset and to gain some sense of the implications of the outcomes. At the start of a transition process, this means investing time to share the purpose and intended outcomes. This also requires providing regular updates on how progress and developments are in alignment with the core purpose and outcomes as the transition journey evolves. The intent is to create a clear holding context for the transition process and provide a tangible benchmark to reduce the risk from the fear of not-knowing what will actually be delivered in practice.

Relationship Being able to see and form connections across a range of different aspects are core needs for relationship capabilities. Showing how the change connects to known practices, the operational and broader organisational strategy creates an integrated context at the outset. Seeking involvement and regular feedback from the workforce encourages and supports people to be engaged and feel connected to the transitional journey as it unfolds. The intent is to reduce the risk of projected fears of people feeling excluded from the transition process and controlled by the outcome.

Expert Understanding the causes and solutions to complex challenges are core needs for expert capabilities. Articulating the core requirements and how the change is aiming to address and solve the organisational challenges creates an informing context at the outset. In practice this requires sharing how complex problems are being overcome and the new potential that is created as the journey unfolds to facilitate ongoing engagement in the execution process. The intent is to reduce the risk of projected fear that the approach and outcomes will not be fit for purpose.

In practice, all of these approaches are useful, particularly for large programmes of work. The key factors to consider are how much emphasis is being placed on the different approaches. To be aware of the concentration of primary and secondary capabilities, ensuring enough resources are available to inform and support the community of the workforce that the change will impact.

Case study 8.3 illustrates how knowing the primary and secondary core capabilities supported how we approached the CRM programme.

Case Study 8.3 CRM Core Capabilities

The outcome from a capability mapping exercise revealed that the primary core capability was Expert. The workforce that would be impacted was people who had depth in knowledge, skills and capabilities of selling retail products. The secondary core capabilities reflected how people approached their sales responsibilities and were a mixture of Expert and Relationship. In practice, this revealed that 65% of the division had developed and utilised their own preferred client relationship methods and approaches (Expert). While the rest of the division utilised building partnerships and depth in internal and external relationships to co-create approaches through collaborating and sharing information (Relationship).

Our findings illuminated the key factors that were at the heart of the division's challenge, we were also mindful that taking and holding a neutral position was going to be crucial to the success of the programme. While there was consistency in what people did (Expert), we would also need to accommodate the differences in the how (Relationship) to facilitate active engagement from within the workforce at the start and throughout the life-cycle of the programme.

Transparency – given Expert capabilities like to understand the causes and solutions to problems, we were aware that we needed to provide detailed information to the whole division. At the start, we attended department meetings to share the programme's purpose and intended approach. We were also mindful that providing accessible detail would be an ongoing task, as the programme evolved. To support expert capability needs, we attended the executive team's weekly meetings to provide progress updates. We worked with the division's communications team to provide bi-weekly summaries that were shared with the whole workforce. We also gave an update of progress at the quarterly divisional meetings, followed by a Q&A session.

Engagement – knowing that those with the secondary preference for relationship would want to connect and relate to the ongoing agenda, we formed a department representative team. What became known as the CRM Rep Team was comprised of volunteers to act as departmental representatives of the programme. The purpose of the CRM Rep Team was to ensure that all departments across the division were actively engaged in shaping the approach and execution of the programme. Our intent was to mitigate any risks of the workforce feeling done to or disconnected from the programme. We also established an open, informal monthly inquiry forum, where we addressed specific detailed questions and invited feedback from the broader workforce population.

Transition Teams

Another unintentional challenge I witness in many organisations is that programmes and projects can develop a life of their own. Splitting themselves off from their environment, until they have developed the solution and then find they have difficulties in getting buy-in or implementing their desired outcomes. Walking the middle path in practice means creating and holding a supportive environment of mutuality at all stages of the transformation process. Regardless of context or programme of work, the more engaged the workforce are at the outset, the more likely they are to support the execution and delivery processes. A helpful way of deploying mutuality strategies is to establish transition teams.

Transition teams can take many forms. They can be utilised at the outset of a programme/project to provide feedback and input on strategy and implementation design. Transition teams can also take the form of steering committees that provide feedback, challenge and support approaches as strategies evolve into practical application. As transformation programmes get underway, transition teams can actively participate in different work streams to support effective strategy execution. Transition teams work best when they are comprised of a mix of members of the core programme/project, volunteers from stakeholders and the workforce. When people volunteer to be part of the change agenda, it facilitates shared understanding, active engagement and collective ownership. Reducing the risks of fundamental aspects being overlooked by the core project team, and people feeling excluded or done to by the outcomes.

Transition teams support programme and project managers to utilise the power in diversity of thought, skills, knowledge and different perspectives to co-design and execute workable solutions. They can also draw on these resources to honour complexity, work with ambiguity as and when inevitable challenges arrive along the transition pathway. In large programmes that consist of a range of different work streams, it can be useful to have a transition team to support each one.

Case study 8.4 shows how a transition team supported the start of the CRM transformation programme.

Case Study 8.4 CRM Start-Up Transition Team
As part of developing a transition strategy and approach, our focus was to leverage and build on the effective practices that were already in place. We were mindful that we did not want to break what was already working and risk introducing more complexity and ambiguity by implementing something new. Our starting point was to understand in-depth the specific differences in the different CRM practices across the division. The questions at the forefront of our minds were what is working/not working and why? We were aware that

how we approached the information gathering exercise would be key to the quality of the data that we collected and the programme as a whole. The frame-of-reference at the forefront of our approach was to mitigate the risk of being seen as objective observers who made positive or negative judgements about the practices of others.

Knowing that splitting of different practices existed across the division, we intended to utilise the data-gathering exercise to begin the process of facilitating an environment of mutuality. Our first transition team was formed to collect data, comprised of two members of the core programme team, an HR representative and volunteer representatives from each of the separate departments. The purpose of the team was to co-create the inquiry methods, collate the data and summarise the findings. The intent was that we would utilise our findings to inform the design and approach of the next phase of the programme.

Adopting Flexibility

The future is a mystery because it is yet to happen, and there are many dimensions that have the potential to influence what comes into the reality of the here and now. Our perspective of the future is a projected reality of what we perceive may happen. While we can plan as much as we like, the reality is that we do not know, what will happen until we are in fully the experience of what Stacey (2001) terms as the living present. The only aspects we can rely on are the qualities and dimensions of our experiences in the current state of the now. In reality this means that whatever we plan or think may happen is subject to a whole host of different dimensions that are likely to evolve over time.

Another frequent challenge that I have witnessed throughout my whole career is an attachment to the plan. How programme/project managers become fixated on the plan and overlook, how they may be required to adjust their activities and approaches as the programme of work evolves. Planning is a helpful practice, as it provides a sense of focus and direction as long as we are willing to adapt, flex and adjust our approaches in line with our current experiences of present.

The transition cycle from Chap. 3 can be a useful planning resource at the outset and during execution of a transition process for providing potential insights into the journey ahead. Although, this does not mean to say that what occurs in practice will happen in the way we expect. I find that the most effective way of dealing with this is to adopt a flexible frame-of-reference. To focus our attention on the aspects that are appearing in the here and now, expecting that whatever we plan about the future will require adjustments as the transitional journey unfolds over time.

Piloting

An approach that supports embracing a flexible approach is piloting. The purpose of running pilots is to explore proof of concept. Piloting is a process of inquiry into what works and does not, supporting the suspension of judgement until there is enough evidence to support a defined plan, path or approach. Particularly in substantial programmes of work, trying and testing out plans, concepts, ideas and approaches before rolling them out to a broader audience can be resourceful to the whole programme of work.

There are many unknowns at the outset and during the execution of transformation programmes. My philosophy is that it is better to have some insight upfront and as the journey evolves than risk the implications of the unknown until we have travelled too far down the wrong pathway. As we begin to translate plans into action, how do we know what was proposed at the outset will actually work in practice until we try it out?

Piloting helps to shed light into unknown territories, creating and facilitating a context of discovery. When we run proof of concept pilots, the explicit message that we send out is flexibility. The notion that plans, concepts and approaches are not fixed or set in stone, they are open to new/different possibilities and potential. Running pilots also transmits the implicit message of mutuality, that programme/project managers are open to active engagement in their transformation agendas. Pilots help with preventing another common transition challenge of trying to eat all of the elephant in one go or biting off more than we can chew at the outset. While initially, this may impact the timeline in the short term, outcomes and benefits outweigh the costs in the long term. Here are a few factors that support effective pilots.

Volunteers As with transition teams, inviting volunteers to participate in a pilot facilitates active engagement. People do not generally tend to volunteer for something if their hearts and minds are not invested in some part of the activity. Depending on the context of the pilot, volunteers can take the form of individuals, intact teams or departments. A key factor to consider is to focus on creating a supportive context and provide freedom of choice in the roles that people undertake while they are participating in the pilot activities.

Confidentiality Exploring proof of concept is a journey into the unknown. We do not know what we will find until we begin to take action. As we have been exploring throughout this book, some people find this exciting and others find this process overwhelming. When we seek voluntary participation in pilots, in practice, we are not judging individuals; we are testing, reviewing and evaluating processes, in alignment with the purpose of the pilot. One way of creating a safe environment for exploration with pilots is to contract for confidentiality at the start of the process. Even if discoveries turn out to be positive, that participants want to be identified with, contracting for confidentiality facilitates a context of safety upfront until we know what we are dealing with.

Involvement When people have been involved in a pilot, they have developed a relationship with the transformation process in some shape or form. Particularly if a pilot has been successful or uncovered insights into potential challenges, offering involvement in the ongoing change agenda can be resourceful to the programme of work as it evolves. Involvement can take the form of people participating in transition teams, to support new workstreams as they emerge or advisory roles, where they have the opportunity to utilise their pilot experiences to contribute to the roll-out of the broader agenda.

Case Study 8.5 CRM Programme Pilots
One of our key findings from the data collection exercise was that some teams had established CRM practices that were effective within their own departmental contexts. With the intent of wanting to incorporate existing best practices, we formed a Core Design team comprised of volunteer representatives from across the division. Incorporating a range of different approaches, the purpose of the design team was to develop an integrated divisional practice. The design team initiated four pilot programmes with intact teams to trial and test out the practical application of amalgamated, policies, processes and procedures. The outcomes from the pilots were utilised to form the basis for the integrated division-wide CRM practice.

Transition Mapping

While the transition cycle can be useful to support the development of a transition strategy at the outset of a change process, it can also be utilised for tracking progress and mitigating the risks of systemic transition overload.

Tracking Progress

As we saw in Chap. 3 with the regulatory project team, lots of activities do not necessarily equate to effective progress and outcomes. Programme and project teams can find that they are putting a lot of time, energy and effort into something and not actually transforming anything in practice. As programmes and projects translate their strategies into actions, the transition cycle can be utilised as a through-time orientation resource for tracking progress and providing insight into some of the subtle signals that often go unnoticed. As a resource for spotting patterns to support effective delivery and provide early warning signals of challenges before they become blockers to progress as the transitional journey unfolds. Once the transition strategy and approach has been formed, I find that it is useful to set some benchmarks; here are a few questions that support the monitoring process.

1. *Key factors* – what specifically do we want to monitor?
2. *Gateways* – how will we know when gateways have been crossed?
3. *Evidence* – what will we need to see to support our findings?
4. *Support* – what specific activities will facilitate the ongoing transition process?
5. *Challenges* – how will we know if progress is stalling?

Case Study 8.6 CRM Progress Tracking
Once the design team had developed the new divisional practice, our focus of attention was on engagement. Knowing at the outset that there were diverse CRM practices, our transitional benchmark was focused on active engagement across the division. Our key question was how many teams would actively engage in the data collection, co-create the design and adopt the new integrated divisional approach? As we were aware that engagement was our benchmark, it was a relatively straightforward process to see who was and was not engaging in the different transitional phases. Our insights prompted the core programme team to know where to focus their efforts in keeping momentum with the pilots that were delivering data and outcomes. The programme team also found that it gave them a heads up of knowing the teams and departments that required additional focus, support and different interventions, to meet the division-wide programme outcomes.

Transition Orientation Mapping

When leaders overlook that the effectiveness of their organisations is reliant on integrated systemic processes of interaction, another unintentional challenge that can emerge is transition overload. By splitting off their change agendas into self-contained categories (people, process, technology) organisations can overlook how many different types of transitions that they are expecting their workforces to embrace. Unnecessary complexity and ambiguity can also be caused by stress and overwhelm of being required to navigate too many different transitions at the same time.

A way of mitigating this risk is to conduct a transition orientation map. To monitor the in-time impact of how many different change agendas are currently influencing the operational system, before starting new programmes. Transition orientation maps can also be utilised as a future pacing resources to support planning and objective setting activities, to mitigate the risks of transitional overload over time. When leaders become aware of how many activities are or likely to be impacting their organisations at any one point in time, it creates a context to pause, question and assess the collective impact. The key question that transition orientation maps raise is what is being asked of the whole organisational system?

When it comes to creating a transition orientation map a useful starting point is to start with associated relevance to gateways. Gateways represent significant transitional milestones and provide insight into potential pressure points.

Interrupting Norms – how many familiar ways of working are being interrupted?
Letting Go – how many known practices are expected to stop and be let go of?
Creating New – how many new/different behaviours and operational practices are required to be developed?

Once leaders have a sense of the impact of the vital transitional milestones, then they have the potential to take a step back, take a realistic view and make some informed choices. Here are some questions that can support a systemic transition review process.

1. What are the crucial change/transformation processes?
2. Is what we are asking of the organisational system realistic in practice?
3. Can any of these be postponed, rescheduled or stopped altogether?

Case study 8.7 illustrates the discoveries that we made in the Retail Sales division at the beginning of the CRM programme.

Case Study 8.7 Retail Sales Division Transition Mapping (Fig. 8.2)

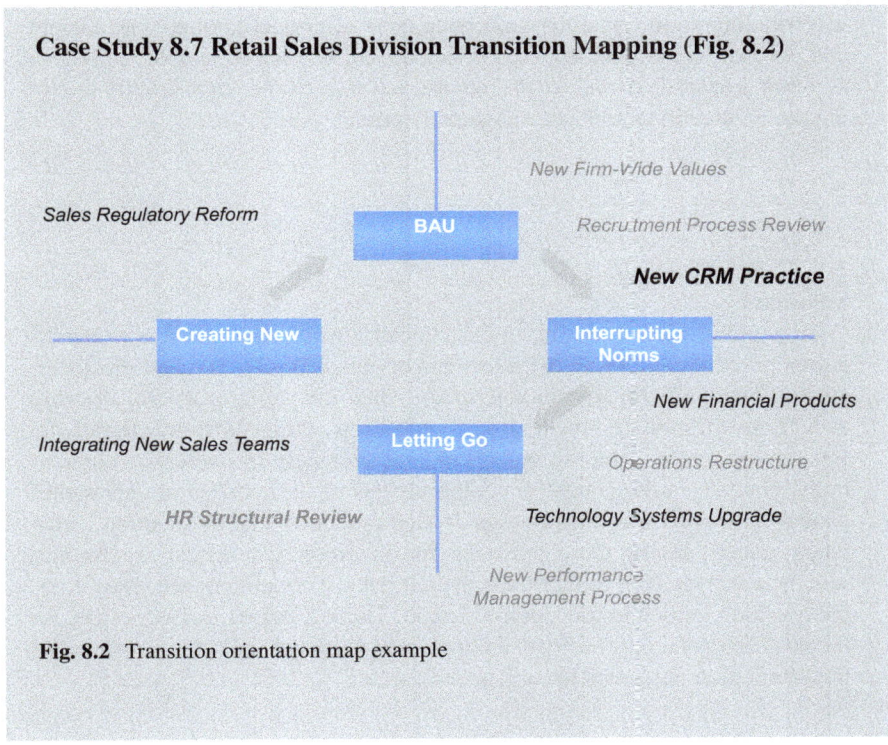

Fig. 8.2 Transition orientation map example

(continued)

Case Study 8.7 (continued)

This systemic overview revealed that there were some core programmes that were underway that were essential. For example, embedding new financial products into the sales portfolio, the trading systems upgrade, integrating new sales teams and adhering to the new regulatory standards. As we reviewed the other programmes of work, we could see that they all had connections with the purpose of the new CRM programme. Rather than treating them as separate individual pieces of work, we collaborated with the key stakeholders for each of the programmes and designed an integrated agenda. We intended to utilise the new CRM programme to create new operational practices that would inform the HR structural, performance management and recruitment reviews. All of these projects were designed to align with the new Firm-Wide values.

While in practice, nothing was stopped, the divisional transition map created a systemic organisational perspective. It supported all programme and project managers to collaborate to create an integrated transitional agenda. The outcomes were that some project deadlines were rescheduled until the broader infrastructures had been built. Rescheduling timelines also meant that we were able to mitigate the associated risks of project failures. Our insight and perspectives gained from the review meant that we were able to create a systemic transitional context for the division as a whole, significantly reducing the unintentional risks of transition overload.

Summary

What we have been exploring in this chapter are essential business risk mitigation practices that support leaders and organisations to navigate the different territories of the transitional space. How clarifying purpose, drawing awareness to splitting, methodology mind-sets, understanding operational functioning and developing transition strategies help to overcome unintentional challenges. Plus, how the combinations of these different approaches contribute to effective transition leadership practices. The proposition is that when leaders deploy these practices and incorporate practical approaches, into their tool kit, they reduce the potential risks of creating unnecessary complexity, ambiguity and transition overload. These different practices increase the potential to facilitate effective transitional journeys and achieve successful transformation outcomes for organisations.

An Invitation for Self-Inquiry

To ground these concepts in practical application, the invitation is to explore how these practices and approaches can support your transition leadership practice. Here are a few questions to support your inquiry:

Purpose

1. What is the purpose of your role, and how does it align with your team, division, department and organisation?
2. How can you utilise purpose statements to support your transition leadership practice?

Mitigating Transitional Risks

Splitting – does this make an appearance in your agenda and what approaches can you take to deploy an integrated approach?

Methodology Mind-Set – do you have a preferred methodology, and how does this shape your focus and actions?

Operational Functioning – do you fully understand the operational functioning that impacts your transition agenda?

Transition Strategies – how do/can you utilise these to support your agenda?

Approaches for Leading Transitions

A Neutral Position – how do/can you walk the middle path?

Core Capabilities – how does your approach align to meet primary and secondary needs?

Transition Teams – how do/can you utilise transition teams to support your agenda?

Flexibility – how do/can you embrace and incorporate flexible practices?

Piloting – how do/can you utilise pilots to support your transition agenda?

Transition Mapping – how can you utilise this to track progress and mitigate systemic overload?

Reference

Stacey, R. (2001). *Complex responsive processes in organizations*. London: Routledge.

Part III
Transition Inquiry Practices

Whether it is individuals, teams or organisations, leading and facilitating any type of transitional process will require some aspect of inquiry. Presented in an applied practitioner context, Part III focuses on resourceful approaches and methods that can be utilised to facilitate effective transition inquiry practices. Chap. 9 focuses on approaches and methods for inquiring with others in organisations and Chap. 10 illustrates processes that support Self-Inquiry. Inquiry practices, that when combined with the approaches from Parts I and II, make valuable contributions to support effective transition leadership practices.

Chapter 9
Inquiry in Organisations

Introduction

A core resource for leading and facilitating effective transitions in organisations is to have insight into the key factors that are influencing and informing operational functioning. Knowing what contributes to how something is functioning provides valuable insight to inform the why, what and how of the transitional journey. Conducting inquiries at the outset of transformation processes provides insights into factors informing the existing landscape. Inquiries can also be utilised to illuminate key factors that will influence the practical implementation of a transition strategy. And as transition processes get underway, inquiring into aspects and dynamics that appear as the journey evolves can provide valuable insights to support transformation processes.

This chapter focuses on how inquiries can provide valuable insights to support the effective design, implementation and facilitation of transition strategies. Presented in an applied practical context, the content focuses on resourceful practices for inquiring with others in organisations. Utilising a focused case study, this chapter provides insights into a range of approaches and methods that can be utilised to support a variety of organisational transitions.

Recognising and Understanding Patterns

Even though our environments are comprised of continuous processes of transitions, an aspect that can be either taken for granted or overlooked is the formation of repeating patterns. Depending on the context, repeating patterns can be enablers and/or disablers of transformation agendas and in organisations these can take many forms. Patterns are formed in processes of thinking, the deployment of skills, knowledge, capabilities and how they inform behaviours and environmental

© Springer Nature Switzerland AG 2020
C. Hayes, *Transition Leadership*, https://doi.org/10.1007/978-3-030-42787-0_9

world-views. Patterns can also show up in repeated practices of how processes, policies and procedures are executed.

What frequently goes unseen is the impact that repeating patterns have on operational functioning and performance of organisations. The core challenge is that repeating patterns are frequently overlooked because they have a tendency to reside outside of individual and collective conscious awareness. For example, we tend to take for granted when things are working well and yet we may not know the specifics of the factors that are informing and contributing to the outcome. Equally, we may know or sense that something is not working and respond by dismissing and avoiding a dysfunctional dynamic without investing time in getting to the bottom of the what, why and how.

The purpose of conducting pattern recognition in organisations is to understand repeating factors that inform the broader systemic context. In practice this means that the patterns we uncover will tend not to exist within a single individual, unless they have something that is totally unique. The focus of inquiry tends to be more about how individuals, teams and groups of functions are contributing to repetitive patterns in the broader functioning of the organisation. I have found that it is particularly helpful to inquire into three primary aspects.

Success Factors

If something is working and delivering outcomes and results, then knowing the repeating factors that are contributing to success generates potential. If we know the what, why and how of a successful repeating pattern then, we can utilise inquiry insights to inform and facilitate how these can be replicated. Understanding factors that contribute to success can be utilised to support specific transitional processes and/or to make broader contributions to an existing environment, and the wider organisational agenda.

Dimensions of Risk

Just because something is not working doesn't mean that it is not worthwhile investing time to conduct and understand why, in fact quite the opposite. If a repeating pattern is present and not contributing to achieving desired outcomes, then it is resourceful to understand the specific elements that are informing the challenge. Knowing the contributing factors that are informing a dysfunctional pattern provides insight and choices in how to work with and mitigate associated risks. Understanding the different dimensions that are creating risk factors can be utilised to enhance operational performance and also to inform the development and implementation of transition strategies.

Known Unknowns

Another aspect that I frequently experience is the known unknowns. These are situations where there is a sense of some kind of repeating pattern taking place that doesn't fall into the success or risk categories. The primary reason is because the pattern is difficult to articulate or describe in straightforward terms. In the context of honouring complexity, just because something is unknown, doesn't mean to say that some or all aspects that are influencing this can't be understood in some capacity. Inquiring into unknown factors can support individuals, teams and organisations to illuminate potential and shine light into darkness. Inquiring into dimensions of known unknowns, supports organisations to gain insight into factors that are influencing the operational system and performance so that they can be worked with.

Knowing Patterns

Gaining insight into patterns of success, risk and dimensions of the unknown has the potential to influence the whole transitional agenda. The key questions to ask are if a pattern keeps repeating itself then what are the dimensions that are reinforcing and keeping it in place? Plus, what influence will repeating patterns have on the transitional agenda?

For example, in the case of the CRM programme in Chap. 8, understanding the different success practices that were informing the operational functioning of the Sales division formed the foundations for the design of the whole programme of work. When James, the technology specialist from Chap. 3, inquired into his own repeating patterns that were risking the effective functioning of his team and division, he could see what actions to take to transform his leadership practices. There is also the example of the unknown practices of the different sales teams in Chap. 7. The lower revenue generating teams were not categorised as risk factors because they were achieving outcomes, their revenues were just not as high as other teams. Once we understood the key patterns in practices and approaches that supported the successful outcomes, then we were able to share them with the broader sales community. This prompted the lower revenue generating teams to inquire into their own practices. Providing the opportunity for team leaders to explore with different team leadership styles that helped to create the environment for facilitating the development of new revenue generating approaches.

Inquiry Perspectives

When conducting inquiries in organisations, my primary focus is to be able to put myself in the shoes of the participants and see through their eyes. To understand how people are thinking and experiencing the world and how their perspectives translate into patterns of behaviour that contribute to outcomes. As Gray (2018) suggests, this is a perspective known as phenomenology in the world of research. The learning from my inquiry practices over the years has revealed that adopting a phenomenological perspective requires reserving our own preconceptions within the field that we are exploring, so that we can fully embrace the context that we are inquiring into.

All processes of inquiry are emergent in nature, what is known in research terms as Progressive (Holiday 2002). As we begin an inquiry we are entering into a transitional process of stepping into the unknown. We won't know the specifics of what we will find at the outset, or what will emerge throughout the journey. The primary reason is because conducting and facilitating inquiries are inherently transitional processes. As with all transitions conducting inquiry is not a linear pathway it is a process of iterative discovery. Whilst conducting and facilitating inquiry processes, I find the most helpful perspective to hold is of being open minded and flexible, to draw awareness to the aspects that emerge as the inquiry process unfolds.

Inquiry Ethics

The way we conduct an inquiry process influences what we uncover and how this will translate into being a supportive transitional resource. A core perspective to keep at the forefront of our mind's eye is that we are inquiring into the patterns of repeating processes not making judgements or pre-empting outcomes, regardless of the context. Our focus is on adopting and maintaining an ethical practice throughout the whole process of inquiry. People don't tend to be forthcoming with engagement in an inquiry process when they feel that they are being judged. Reactions to perceptions of being judged will interrupt the inquiry agenda and the quality of the information that we obtain. Whilst in practice there is the principle that purely by being involved in the inquiry process then we will influence and impact outcomes in some way. A perspective that aligns to what McTaggart (1997) describes as *'Participatory Action Research'* (PAR). Our goal is to be seen and experienced throughout the inquiry process to the best of our abilities to be the neutral facilitators of inquiry. To help achieve this goal there are a number of actions we can take to establish and support an ethical inquiry practice.

Neutrality

Regardless of context, conducting any type of inquiry requires taking and holding a neutral position at the outset and throughout the whole lifecycle of the process. A helpful frame-of-reference is to adopt an inquiring mind, and hold curiosity at the forefront of our intent and actions. Holding and sustaining neutrality requires the qualities of listening, suspending judgement and reserving interpretation that we covered in Chap. 8. The focused intent is on being willing to engage with and be accepting of what we uncover and discover throughout our inquiry process, whether our findings are positive or negative. At the end of the day any data that we collect about what informs repeating patterns in the environment will be of value and resourceful to support our transition agenda in some shape or form.

Transparency

Being open about our intent and discoveries is key to support the engagement of sponsors and participants. Even if the sponsors and participants are actively bought into the concept, adopting an ethical approach still requires us as inquirers to be transparent about our intent at the outset and the discoveries as they emerge. We can demonstrate transparency by:

At the Outset
- Clearly articulating the purpose of the inquiry in straightforward terms
- Providing information on the potential benefits of the inquiry process (sponsors, participants and the broader workforce community)
- Outlining inquiry approaches and methods
- Providing indications of key requirements and time commitments from both sponsors and participants

During the Inquiry Process
- Providing regular progress updates
- Sharing findings as they emerge throughout the inquiry journey

Confidentiality

Regardless of what we are inquiring into and whether we are working with individuals or teams, creating a context of safety is essential. This applies at the start and throughout the whole process of inquiry. We can co-create and facilitate a context of safety by:

- Supporting individuals to know that their personal identities will be protected
- Clearly stating that participation is voluntary and that individuals have the option of withdrawing at any stage of the process
- Articulating our intentions at the outset of what are we intending on doing with our findings as and when they emerge

Mutuality

A key factor to be mindful of is that we are facilitating a collaborative partnership of inquiring with others as opposed to on others. An approach to research that Heron (1996) terms as Cooperative Inquiry. We can facilitate mutuality in our inquiry practice through:

- Establishing and building partnerships with sponsors and participants
- Seeking volunteers to participate in all or some stages of the inquiry process
- Inviting participants to be involved in the inquiry design process
- Validating findings and key themes with participants as they emerge throughout the inquiry journey
- Inviting participants to participate in the preliminary and final data consolidation exercises

Inquiry Approaches

Given the nature of complexities that underpin and inform the operational functioning in organisations, I find that qualitative approaches tend to be best fit for purpose. This is because they lend themselves to exploratory, emergent and unstructured approaches that can support depth of inquiry into the complex dynamics of human functioning. I have utilised qualitative practices to gain insight and understanding into motivations, attitudes, patterns in thinking, emotional and physical feelings that inform behaviours and outcomes in organisations. Quantitative approaches can be useful, for example, whilst designing surveys although the findings are more resourceful when the topics of inquiry are backed up by qualitative questions.

As with all transition leadership practices, it helps to draw on and blend a range of different approaches and methods depending on the context of inquiry. What follows are the approaches and methods that I have and continue to utilise in my own transition leadership practice.

Action Research

A term established by Lewin in 1946, action research is an approach that focuses on improving social behaviour and facilitating change and transformation. This is an approach where inquiry is systemic in nature, conducted within complex natural social settings built around co-created collaborative partnerships with the researcher and participants. The general principle of action research is that it is an experimental approach that starts with limited information, built on a spiral process of planning, acting, observing and reflecting. The expectations are that an action research inquiry will consist of a number of repeated iterative cycles to refine and validate findings before outcomes are established.

Grounded Theory

Grounded theory was originally created by Glasser and Strauss (1967); its primary purpose is to ground a perspective (theory) in the context within which it occurs. Grounded theory is an approach for generating a perspective (theory) through collecting data, analysing and validating the findings with others. Grounded theory lends itself to an emergent fluid process that aligns with the unknown dimensions of the transitional landscape. At the outset, we won't know what we will find; our insights are gained through what we discover from the emerging patterns in the information and data that we collect. Adopting a grounded theory approach is a useful process that can often uncover a whole range of patterns consisting of a number of different iterations, before we settle on a clearly defined outcome.

Design Principles

In practice, embracing action research and grounded theory approaches will have implications on the design of the inquiry process. Whilst we may start the inquiry with a preliminary design as we engage others, collect data, analyse and validate our findings, it is likely that we may end up adjusting our intended plan and taking a different pathway. Inquiry journeys are emergent, by nature they take the form of a series of iterations that will require shifts in perspectives, design approaches and often a number of redesigns along the way.

Initiating Inquiry

Whilst the process of conducting an inquiry is emergent, we also have to start somewhere. As we initiate an inquiry, clarifying the why, what and how of our intent and initial approach creates the boundaries of what is inside and outside of the process of inquiry. In practice what we are doing is creating an inquiry context and framework to launch and focus our initial activities. These are the three core questions that I utilise to inform the beginning of an inquiry process:

1. Why are we conducting this inquiry?
2. What specifically are we inquiring into?
3. How are we intending to start the inquiry process?

These questions frame our inquiry process and create the context for the information that we provide to our sponsors and participants. Case study 9.1 illustrates how these questions were utilised to initiate the inquiry into the different sales and trading revenue generation practices in Chap. 7.

Case Study 9.1 Revenue Generation Inquiry
1. *Why are we conducting this inquiry?*
   To understand the practices contributing to high revenue generation, so that they can be utilised to support the effective performance of the whole division
2. *What specifically are we inquiring into?*
   The patterns of behaviour that inform different revenue generation practices and approaches
3. *How are we intending to start the inquiry process?*
   Interviews with a sample of sales team leaders

Inquiry Methods

When it comes to inquiring into the complex dynamics of operational functioning, my philosophy is that there is no one methodological approach. Conducting a comprehensive and thorough inquiry requires drawing from a range of different methods for collecting data and validating findings.

Interviewing

As Seidman (2013) suggests, the purpose of interviewing is to gain insight into the lived experiences of others. At the beginning of conducting an inquiry interviewing processes can be used for gathering information about, knowledge, preferences, world-views, values and perspectives that contribute to events, that all inform behavioural practices. As inquiry processes get underway, interviews can also be useful for clarifying, testing emerging themes, consolidating and validating findings. There is a wide range of different interviewing approaches; the type we choose will depend on the purpose that informs our context of inquiry. In adopting a progressive, exploratory emergent approach, particularly for large-scale inquiries, it is useful to start wide and consolidate the focus of inquiry as the journey unfolds. The interview methods that align with this approach are known in research terms as non-directive, semi-structured and focused.

Non-directive

Non-directive interview processes are exploratory and emergent in nature; they can be utilised to deepen inquiry into a specified topic. As interviewers, our focus of attention is placed on the primary purpose of our inquiry, not on definitive answers to specific questions. I find it helpful to start with a high-level question and be open to what emerges.

Case study 9.2 illustrates the non-directive question that framed the start of the inquiry journey into the different sales and trading revenue generation practices.

Case Study 9.2 Revenue Generation Non-directive Interviews
Our initial objective at the outset of our inquiry into the different sales teams was to see if there were any definitive patterns in practices. Bearing in mind at the time we didn't know who were high and low revenue generating teams, as we began our inquiry with 15 different team leaders, the question that framed our inquiry was:
   In your view, what contributes to high revenue generation?

Semi-Structured

Semi-structured interview processes are framed around a particular context, where we can have a range of questions that may or not be answered. We may also find that as the interview processes get underway, more information and questions emerge that open up new pathways of exploration.

Case study 9.3 shows the questions that formed the framework for semi-structured interviews that were utilised to focus the revenue generation inquiry process.

Case Study 9.3 Revenue Generation Semi-Structured Interviews
After gaining a range of perspectives from the different sales team leaders these were the questions that supported us to frame the focus of our next stage of inquiry:

1. *How does your team generate revenue?*
2. *What key factors contribute to this?*
3. *How would you describe your team leadership practice?*

Focused

As themes emerge and we begin to uncover more information and gain greater insights, focused interviews into specified topics can provide depth and consolidation of themes to our inquiry process.

Case study 9.4 shows the focused questions that supported us to deepen our inquiry and gain more specific information about the different sales practices.

Case Study 9.4 Revenue Generation Focused Interviews
1. *How do you tend to approach the market?*
2. *Do you have any particular strategies for how you work with clients?*
3. *How is your team structured?*
4. *Do you have any specific team operational processes or policies?*
5. What would you say are the key success factors of your team?

Behavioural Events

Behavioural events are another form of focused interview process and a method that is particularly helpful for when we are trying to gain detailed insights into a particular topic. Behavioural event interviews can provide insight into thoughts, feelings, motivations, skills and knowledge that inform behaviours relating to a particular scenario or event. This method is also useful for understanding key competencies and can provide detailed insights into how individuals conduct their work.

Case study 9.5 shows the questions that supported us to understand the different practices for how people developed relationships.

Case Study 9.5 Revenue Generation Behavioural Event Interviews
As our inquiry into the different practices of the sales teams unfolded, a theme that kept reoccurring was that there were different perspectives on how people developed relationships. We became curious to see if there were any specific competences or practices that contributed to how people approached their relationships with clients and their colleagues. These were the questions that supported us to gain insights into behaviours of the different team practices:

1. *How do you approach your relationships?*
2. *How do you maintain existing relationships?*
3. *What approach do you take to developing new relationships?*
4. *Do you see any differences between internal and external relationships?*
5. *What impact do the relationships within your team have on revenue?*

Focus Groups

These are interviews conducted with a group of people about a particular subject matter. The purpose of focus groups is to build the context of co-creating processes of exploration through dialogue and exploration. Focus groups can be used at the beginning to generate avenues for inquiry during the data collection processes to deepen understanding or to validate findings. I tend to find they are most productive when they are comprised of between four and eight participants. Primarily because, less than four, we narrow the potential that can be gained from diverse perspectives; more than eight, we risk introducing too much diversity and then data can be difficult to capture. Focus groups can be comprised of intact teams or a range of different individuals, depending on the topic of inquiry.

Case study 9.6 shows how focus groups were utilised to share emerging themes and deepen our understanding of our findings.

Case Study 9.6 Revenue Generation Focus Groups

We utilised focus groups to share patterns that were emerging and deepen our understanding of the different relationship practices with the people who participated in the different interview processes. Whilst at the time we still didn't know who were high or lower generation teams, we were starting to get a sense of the practices and approaches that contributed to successful outcomes. These were the key points that we shared with one focus group that turned out to represent the high revenue generating practices.

Market Approaches – ambiguity creates potential for new/different solutions
Primary Strategies – revenue generated through internal/external partnerships
Leadership Practices – facilitating mutuality, utilising diversity, challenge complacency, collective decision-making
Team Structure – all members considered equal, collective accountabilities and responsibilities
Operational Processes – information shared through two-way dialogue
Relationships – building trusting partnerships with team members, colleagues and clients

---

Observations

Observations are useful for testing out hypothesis and deepening understanding of the constructs of themes as they emerge to support the process of validating findings. One key factor to be mindful of is that when we are conducting observations, the sheer nature of our presence will influence our inquiry. An approach for mitigating associated risks of our physical presence is to be transparent, without intentions. Practicing transparency when conducting observations requires clearly articulating the purpose and the specifics of what we are intending to observe at the outset of inquiry with the participants who are directly involved in the process.

My personal preference is to conduct an observation exercise in the context of mutuality with people who have developed some form of relationship with the inquiry process. This reduces the risk of us as inquirers introducing unnecessary fear or being perceived as the objective observers who are there to make judgements. Due to the evolving iterative nature of inquiry processes it is highly likely that at the outset we won't know when or where we may want to utilise observations. Being transparent about our unknowns and that observations may play a part at the outset, of an inquiry is another useful risk mitigation approach.

Case study 9.7 shows how we used observations to gain first hand experiences and begin the process of validating our findings.

Case Study 9.7 Revenue Generation Observations
After running the focus groups, we were mindful that we had uncovered core themes about the patterns in the different sales practices. Our curiosity was drawn towards how these patterns showed up in the day-to-day practical realities of the different teams. Our next step was to immerse ourselves in the environments of different sales teams to establish first hand experiences of participating in high and low revenue generation practices. Operating as a duo of two co-inquirers my colleague and I conducted observation exercises of ten teams over a period of two weeks. Contracting to be regarded as temporary staff, we spent a day with each team sitting on the sales floor putting ourselves in the shoes of participant team members.

Online Surveys

In a transition inquiry practice conducting online surveys can have several purposes. To gain input and insight from a broader audience, draw awareness to a specific topic of inquiry, engage and give the workforce a voice. Some organisations have their own preferred software for collecting data. There are also other software products and tools like Qualtrics, SurveyMonkey, Survey Gizmo and Survey Writer that can be utilised to support the data collection process. If you find that conducting an online survey will be useful to support an inquiry process then there are a few principles to take into account.

Context – Prior to launching a survey, invest time in creating an inquiry context and preparing the target audience. Creating context involves sharing the purpose of the survey, what the data will be used for and a general timeline of when the participants will be able to see the findings, recommendations and associated next steps.

Confidentiality – As with all data collection methods if we are asking a broader audience to participate in a survey, then contracting for confidentiality is essential. The core principle being that in conducting a survey, we are interested in broader patterns and perspectives on the topic of inquiry not the specifics of what one person alone has to say. Plus, if people know that their individual identities are respected then there are more likely to be forthcoming and open in their responses.

Specificity – Being clear at the outset about the data we want to collect and utilising this to inform the specific questions we want to ask provides the most resourceful outcomes. Specificity in practice means investing time to articulate clear and direct questions and validate these with a sample of the intended audience prior to launching the survey.

Case study 9.8 shows how we utilised an online survey to gain additional data

---

Case Study 9.8 Revenue Generation Online Survey

By conducting the observation exercise as inquirers, we had made our presence known to the broader sales community. Team members who were not involved in the interviews or focus groups yet wanted to be more involved and make a contribution to our inquiry process. We were also mindful that when our inquiry was completed that we would need an avenue for engaging the workforce in sharing our findings and a platform to launch recommendations. Given that we were low on resources, conducting an online survey seemed like the most appropriate way forward to collect new data, engage the workforce and create the foundations for sharing different approaches and practices.

The outcomes from our observations revealed a wealth of insights about the variations of the different team practices across the division. One key theme was the differences in how the teams approached the external environment and the impact that this had on their commercial focus. These were the commercial focus questions that formed part of our online survey:

Commercial Focus

1. On a scale of 1–6 how do you rate your team's commercial focus?

Very ineffective 1 2 3 4 5 6 Very effective

   If *very effective*, what specifically makes your team's commercial focus successful?
   If *ineffective*, how do you think your commercial focus could be improved?

2. How do you currently generate revenue?
3. How can you increase your revenue generation?
4. What is your team's competitive advantage?
5. What challenges do you face in generating more revenue?

---

from a broader audience and engage the workforce, with the revenue generation inquiry.

Data Collection and Validation

How we collect data, analyse and validate findings will have a major impact on the credibility of our outcomes and how our inquiry communities engage with our recommendations. While collecting and validating data it is useful to apply adopt a few core principles:

Triangulation

One of the reasons why I like to utilise a range of methods and approaches is that they provide options and different lenses to deepen inquiry into a particular subject. If we can demonstrate that a repeating pattern can be illustrated through a range of different data collection methods then we can show rigour in our approach. This means that the themes and patterns that emerge in our inquiry are derived from multiple sources, providing depth and credibility to the findings.

Sampling

My experiences of selecting sample sizes are that they are a balancing act. The primary focus is about making sure that the target population is adequately representative of the topic of inquiry. At the same time, being mindful of trying not incorporating too many examples that finding consistent patterns and themes in the data can become over complicated with too many variables. In selecting sample sizes for interviews, at the beginning of the inquiry process, a reasonable range is between 8 and 15 participants. These numbers can then be expanded as and when required as the inquiry journey unfolds. With regards to focus groups, it is useful to have one focus group aligned to a particular topic or avenue of inquiry at the start and then create more as and when new themes emerge.

Data Collection Approach

With individuals and teams, I am a big fan of being open with my data collection process. Whilst conducting interviews and focus groups, flipcharts and whiteboards are useful so that the participants can see the data that that is being collected. This approach holds the facilitator to account for how they are interpreting what people are saying. Also, if something is overlooked or misinterpreted, it creates an open context for the participants to contribute to the accuracy of the data. Whilst conducting observations, if notes are taken, then time permitting, it is resourceful to share these with the participants at the end of the exercise. If there are time constraints, then an alternative option is to offer to schedule a separate session, suspending any analysis until the notes have been shared and the information obtained has been clarified with participants.

Data Analysis

Pattern recognition doesn't just apply to initiating a process of inquiry; it also forms the basis for analysing the data that we collect. When analysing data, if a consistent theme appears and/or a factor repeats itself then its worthy of exploration. This generally makes an appearance in language patterns, where the same phrases or words are consistently repeated, within a given context. Exploring patterns in data also has another useful purpose. If we have used a range of different data collection methods, and the same patterns appear in different contexts. then its shows validity in our findings. In addition, if no more new or different patterns emerge then it is a signal for knowing when to stop.

Case study 9.9 illustrates the key language patterns that emerged through interviews, focus groups, observations and the online survey.

> **Case Study 9.9 Revenue Generation Language Patterns**
> The key definitive words that informed the sales team inquiry were plural versus singular descriptions. In the teams that were built on a collective mutuality focus the words "we, our, us" were repeatedly reported. Versus the teams that were founded on an individual focus the words, "me, I, one," were more prominent.

> **Case Study 9.10 Revenue Generation Summary of Findings**
> In the process of summarising our findings we were able to show the differences between individual and collective based practices by clearly articulating how the consistent language patterns of "we, our, us' and "me, I, one," showed up in:
>
> • Market Approaches
> • Primary Strategies
> • Leadership Practices

(continued)

Case Study 9.10 (continued)

- Team Structures
- Operational Processes
- Internal and External Relationships

Whilst presenting our findings to the sponsors and participants we were able to provide the consolidated framework that consisted of the practical examples provided in Table 7.1 in Chap. 7.

Summary
What we have been exploring in this chapter are the different approaches and methods for conducting inquiries in organisations. How practices of recognising patterns, adopting emergent approaches and inquiring with others can be utilised to support a wide range of organisational transitions. The key principles being that when inquiry is incorporated as part of the transition leadership practice, the outcomes provide valuable insights to support effective design, implementation and facilitation of transition strategies.

An Invitation for Self-Inquiry
If you are interested in incorporating inquiries into your transition leadership practice, then here are a few questions to consider:

Pattern Recognition
Successes

- What is currently successful and working well?
- Are there any known factors that are contributing to this?

Risks

- Are there any factors that are not working or dysfunctional?
- What aspects are informing this?

Unknowns

- Are there any known unknowns within your agenda?
- If so what impact are they having?

Conducting Inquiry
Ethics

- How do you demonstrate these in your inquiry practice?

Approaches

- What approaches are best fit for purpose to support your inquiry practice?

Methods

- What range of methods can you utilise to support your inquiry practice?

Data Collection and Validation

- How can you utilise triangulation to illustrate rigour in your inquiry?
- What approaches can support you to collect data?
- How are you incorporating pattern recognition in your data analysis?
- What approaches can you take to share and present your findings?

Presenting Findings

When sharing our findings, with others it helps to show an audit trail of what we have uncovered and where we have found it. We can also develop credibility by describing the key patterns that have informed our inquiry and explaining their applied practical impact.

Case study 9.10 shows the structure that we chose to illustrate how the individual and collective approaches appeared in multiple contexts in the practices of the different teams.

Study Tip 9.1
If you are studying and/or interested in gaining greater depth into research methods and approaches in this chapter, Gray's (2018) 'Doing Research in the Real World' is one of the most accessible texts. It provides a comprehensive view of the field of conducting practitioner and academic research projects supported by wide range of case studies and practical examples.

References

Glasser, B. G., & Strauss, A. L. (1967). *The discovery of grounded theory: Strategies for qualitative research*. Chicago: Aldine de Gruyter.

Gray, D. E. (2018). *Doing research in the real world*. Los Angeles: Sage.

Heron, J. (1996). *Cooperative inquiry: Research into the human condition*. London: Sage.

Holiday, A. (2002). *Doing and writing qualitative research*. London: Sage.

McTaggart, R. (1997). Guiding principles for participatory action research. In R. McTaggart (Ed.), *Participatory action research*. Albany: State University of New York Press.

Seidman, I. (2013). *Interviewing as qualitative research: A guide for researchers in education and the social sciences* (4th ed.). New York: Teachers College Press.

Chapter 10
Conducting Self-Inquiry

Introduction

A theme carried throughout this book is that the practice of self-inquiry is at the heart of leading successful transitions. We have been working with the principles that navigating the different complexities of the transitional space requires knowing the nature of the relationship we have with transition experiences. Leaders find that having insight into the different facets of self-self relationships provides resources to support the effectiveness of their transition leadership practices.

Adopting a practice of self-inquiry is a dynamic cyclical process. It is a practice that supports exploration into patterns of thinking, emotions, skills, knowledge and physical symptoms that influence ways of being with transitions. Self-inquiry can be utilised to gain insight into core human aspects that inform behaviours, the nature of the relationships that we have with others, the environment and ourselves.

Framed around a personal case study of transforming a challenging relationship with writing, this chapter illustrates methods and approaches that facilitate effective self-inquiry practices. Practices of self-inquiry that supports leaders to navigate and work with the inner complex territories of their transitional experiences.

In-Time Inquiry

If you have been working with the exercises in each chapter, then you have been engaging in a form of self-inquiry. If you have related some of your responses to previous experiences, then you have adopted what Dewey (1910) terms as a reflective practice.

When faced with an unknown aspect or transitional challenge, I find that it is useful to begin the reflective process with an in-time inquiry. Conducting in-time inquiries provides support in drawing awareness to the range of aspects that are

© Springer Nature Switzerland AG 2020
C. Hayes, *Transition Leadership*, https://doi.org/10.1007/978-3-030-42787-0_10

informing our experiences of the present. In-time inquiries can be utilised to gain insight into the qualities, patterns and nature of the relationships that are forming and informing our sense-of-self in any given moment. For example, we may say we like or dislike something and yet if we do not invest time in understanding the dimensions that are informing our inner experiences then it can often be difficult to leverage the benefits or transform our challenges.

The outcomes from in-time inquiry processes can provide awareness to the multifaceted dimensions of our self-self relationships that inform the nature of the relationships we have with our transitional experiences.

The practice of conducting an in-time inquiry is comprised of three stages:

Stage 1 – drawing awareness to the elements and impact of our current experience
Stage 2 – analysing and reflecting on patterns and the impact of outcomes
Stage 3 – establishing the focus of our transitional development journey

In-Time Inquiry Stage 1

There are five key questions that help to facilitate Stage 1 of an in-time inquiry process. It is useful to capture responses either in handwritten form or electronically so that they can be utilised for points of reference or further inquiry a later date.

Experience – what is happening?
Qualities – how am I thinking, feeling, sensing this experience?
Influences – what is informing and contributing to the qualities of the experience?
Past – is there anything familiar about this experience, or is it new?
Outcomes – what impact is this experience having on Self, others or the environment?

Case study 10.1 illustrates the context that was created for a self-inquiry process into my relationship with writing after completing Stage 1.

Case Study 10.1 Stage 1 – Exploring a Relationship with Writing
One of the major transitions that I have had to navigate to be able to write this book has been the nature of my relationship with writing. I was aware that it would not be possible to share and bring this research and transition practices into a broader social context if I didn't. Despite receiving positive feedback from a broad range of colleagues on written outcomes over the years, my challenge has always been the nature of the self-self relationship with the process of writing. These were the outcomes from Stage 1 of my in-time inquiry 12 months prior to beginning the process of writing this textbook.

Experience – I am forcing myself to write despite how much I despise it
Qualities – my head, feels like it is locked in a safe, encased in a thick black woollen blanket. My neck and back are tight and stiff. My energy feels like

> it is stuck behind thick wooden shutters that stop it connecting with the
> sunlight. Every time I write, it drains my life force.
> *Influences* – sitting at my desk, shut off from the world, with no mutually
> informing dialogue or connections with others. I am forced to listen to the
> sound of my own voice.
> *Past/Present* – for as long as I can remember, I have always detested writing.
> Each time I write, I get the same physical stiff sensations that result in
> headaches, tiredness and often exhaustion. Even the thought of walking up
> Everest seems like a much more appealing experience than writing.
> *Outcomes* – when I do have to engage in writing, the time invested is kept to
> a minimum, this means I tend to write short topical papers rather than
> large texts. The outcome is that the distribution of my practice and research
> focuses on MBA workshops and consulting projects. It is not supporting a
> broader society to understand and work with the complexities of organisa-
> tional transitions that has become my whole life's vocational purpose.

In-Time Inquiry Stage 2

The outcomes from Stage 1 frame the context and provide valuable points of reference to deepen our inquiry process. The information we obtain can support access
to unseen aspects of our self-relationship providing valuable points of reference to
explore further. Moving into Stage 2 of an in-time inquiry we deepen the process of
self-exploration by drawing awareness to three key aspects:

Known – dimensions that are known and understood
New – anything new, different or surprising
Unknown – elements that cannot be put into words and clearly articulated

Case study 10.2 shows the insights I gained from deepening my inquiry after
completing Stage 2.

Case Study 10.2 Stage 2 – Relationship with Writing Discoveries
In reviewing the responses to Stage 1, what was known and understood was
that I was forcing myself to write. I was also aware of the impact it had on my
physical and emotional state. The new information that unveiled itself from
Stage 2 was that physical and emotional states were influenced by loneliness,
not being able to relate to others and feeling forced to listen to my internal
dialogue. What was unknown was 'why' I had always had a life-long challenge with writing. My challenging relationship with writing was something
that I had accepted and taken for granted. Writing was an activity that I had
avoided by adopting a move away from strategy and kept to a minimum for
the whole of my adult life.

In-Time Inquiry Stage 3

Our reflections and insight gained from Stage 2 can facilitate the potential for development and transformation. Once armed with a greater depth of insight into our lived experiences, we can focus our attention on determining the next steps for action. In some instances, the development pathway can be clear. In other instances, there may be several complex dynamics associated with the self-self relationship that may require further inquiry. This is where the transition cycle that we explored in Chap. 3 can also be utilised as an additional resource for framing and establishing a self-transitional development journey.

Phase 1 Shifting – what will need to be dismantled and deconstructed?
Interrupting Norms – what familiar aspects with require interrupting?
Phase 2 Ending – what will be required to be disintegrated and dissolved?
Letting Go – what known aspects will be required to go?
Phase 3 Emerging – what will require reforming or reconstructing?
Creating New – what new mind-sets, behaviours or practices will be required?
Phase 4 – what will require development?

Case study 10.3 illustrates how utilising the transition cycle to reflect on my insights from Stage 2 facilitated the development journey of transforming my relationship with writing.

Case Study 10.3 Stage 3 – Relationship with Writing Transition
Insights from Stage 2 clarified that the key to transforming my relationship with writing resided in knowing what had contributed to the painful lifelong pattern. It was a pattern that I had just taken for granted and accepted for so many years. The question at the forefront of my mind's eye was what? What specifically had happened that despite many attempts to try different approaches, I could not shake off the physical and mental torture that appeared every time I sat down to write?

Given that I could not answer this question, what became clear was that I had embodied the cause, it resided somewhere in my unconsciousness, inaccessible to the conscious awareness of my cognitive mind. Given that the process of writing had such a profound impact, on my sense-of-self, I sensed that it was somehow related to a past trauma. That somewhere in the past, I had a traumatic experience that had created a negative mind and body relationship with writing that needed uncovering before I could resolve and heal the trauma. I could not frame or map my transitional journey because I did not know the cause of my trauma. The focus of developing a new self-self relationship with writing was going to require accessing and healing some aspect of my self-self relationship that was outside of conscious awareness. These insights opened up a whole new avenue of what I have come to term as embodied self-inquiry.

Embodied Inquiry

Sometimes, no matter how deeply we inquire into the complex dynamics of our self-self relationships, there can be elements that sit outside of our conscious awareness. As my in-time inquiry revealed, we can ask a whole range of different questions, and yet we cannot always open the door to reveal what our body and unconscious mind is keeping tightly locked shut. If we are getting in our own way or having difficulties with an aspect of ourselves that we cannot reveal or resolve, then adopting an embodied inquiry practice can be resourceful.

The purpose of conducting embodied inquiry is to gain access into the complex interconnected aspects of the processes in our mind and body relationships. Conducting an embodied Inquiry is a resourceful approach for drawing awareness to the different constructs in our ways of being in the world. The different constructs that we can unknowingly take for granted, that form and inform our living world experiences.

Journaling

A method that is useful to support gaining access to different aspects of our embodied self-self relationship is journaling. There are many perspectives on the positive benefits of journaling. For example, from a cognitive functioning point of view, it can help with clarifying thoughts, processing, retaining and retrieving information, increasing creativity, stretching and increasing our IQ. There is also the positive impact it can have on supporting mental wellbeing through improving emotional intelligence, expressing and coping with emotional overwhelm, managing anxiety, reducing stress and supporting mood stability. As Pennebaker and Beall (1986), suggest, journaling can be utilised for confronting and healing a trauma or challenging responses to a particular event. As a resourceful practice for creating a sense of inner stability when our external environment feels like it is in total chaos. There are also physiological and physical benefits like strengthening our immune system and enhancing our sleep that all contribute to general wellbeing.

As I discovered through my in-time inquiry, we can get used to our internal dialogue, and do not often see the repeating loops and patterns that reside within the nature of our self-self relationships. Putting it out onto paper, whether it's handwritten or typed acts like a mirror reflecting aspects that we can often keep hidden from our consciousness. Journaling is a process that can be utilised for gaining access to knowing our embodied experiences. As Richardson (2000) advocates, writing is a helpful method for gaining insights and understanding ourselves.

There is a wide range of different journaling methods; the approach that I have found the most useful and adapted to support my practice aligns with some of the principles of Turner-Vesselago's (2013) Freefall Writing process.

1. *Write What Emerges* – begin without planning and go with the topic that emerges through the process of writing. Going with what emerges is an approach that creates the context for our embodied Self to find its own agenda and not be led by the power of thinking mind alone. The key factor is trusting that we will eventually find ourselves walking an interconnected pathway and accessing the topics that truly matter to our interconnected embodied Self.

2. *Write Continuously for Ten Minutes* – do not stop. Resist the urge to correct spelling or typos just keep the flow of the writing process going until the time is up. The purpose of continuous writing is to hold the context and keep the connection with the embodied Self. If we stop to read what we have written or correct our spelling, then we lose the process of our interrelated embodied connection. We reside in and give power to our cognitive minds. This means that we are putting ourselves in the position of judging the outputs that takes us out of the process of being fully in the moment, with our mind/body relational experiences. This process can be particularly challenging if we are typing and the red line of 'bad spelling' appears to prompt us that we have made a typo. Turning off the spell-checking facility helps. Plus being mindful of the purpose of this exercise, that we are doing this to help ourselves. It does require residing in our willpower to focus on the process of writing and keep going; it is only for ten minutes.

3. *Provide Specific Details* – include physical sensations, emotional responses, reactions, the different voices and dialogues that emerge. One of the many unknowns is how we have registered, constructed and stored our experiences over time. We may find that drawing awareness to emotional responses and physical sensations about a particular topic, unveil and provide access to a whole new avenue of meaning. Providing details allows what is there to reveal itself within its own context.

4. *Lean Towards the Energy* – whether it is positive or negative; another key aspect is to lean towards where there is an energetic charge or pull. My philosophy on energy is that it represents meaning and connection to or with something. When we allow ourselves to relate and connect with our embodied energy, it holds the potential for gaining access to aspects that are providing or taking resources, opening up pathways for establishing connections and understanding. For example, if we are happy about something, revealing the factors that are informing our positive experience can provide valuable insights that hold the potential for our happiness to be replicated. Equally, if we are angry, given that anger is a derivative of hurt, unveiling our wounding can facilitate the opportunity for healing and letting go.

Tips for Starting

Initially, when we begin the practice of journaling, it requires self-discipline to establish a few core principles:

Making Time – schedule ten minutes every day for a minimum of four weeks. That may sound a long time. Although the thing to keep at the forefront of awareness is like establishing all new skills, it is a process of developing a new pattern. Developing new patterns requires disciplining ourselves. Making time to create a consistent daily routine creates and facilitates a supportive holding context for establishing a new practice.

Embracing Patience – as we allow a new practice to emerge, it can take some time to connect with the integrated mind/body processes of our embodied Self. It is highly likely that seeing results will not be instantaneous. I discovered that it was useful just to be patient and allow the process of embodied inquiry to unfold within in its own time.

Self-Compassion – when we see our inner world represented on paper or screen; initially, it can reveal surprising aspects that may also evoke experiences of self-consciousness. A useful perspective to keep at the forefront of our awareness is self-compassion. It is about being mindful that journaling is a supportive resource. Self-inquiry is not about making the outcomes a good read for anyone else. This process is your private place to explore, uncover, say and discuss whatever you want.

Following the journaling principles for two weeks of daily practice, case study 10.4 is the journal entry of the self-self dialogue that revealed the origins of my difficult relationship with writing.

Case Study 10.4 Knowing the Relationship with Writing
"Why Is Writing So Painful?"

Being educated. The term says it all. Writing has always been about pleasing others regardless of your needs. Being forced to learn boring topics of Science, Geography, Religious Education, History and then being examined, judged and criticised for how you represented understanding in what you were not interested in learning at the time.

I was not seen or engaged with for being me. I felt treated like an object, judged and evaluated by the controlling teachers against what they wanted to see, not how I had interpreted their subjects. Unlike Art, Drama, Dance and Needlework that were creative and encouragingly supported through relationships and interaction.

Being me was not sitting in a classroom, absorbing information; being me was creating through action and testing out my experiences through applying my learning in practice, not just absorbing and regurgitating concepts and theory. Creating new and different through painting and drawing pictures of beautiful natural subjects and expressing myself through acting and dancing with others, developing tapestries with bright, vibrant colours. I was forced into making myself fit into a context of something without any say or choice.

And then came the line manager feedback in 1990, "keep it snappy, why use 20 words Catherine when two will do?" Death by PowerPoint, I was encouraged to condense vast amounts of information onto three slides so that others could quickly understand the information and messages that I was trying to convey.

In the beginning, the process of writing was not a creative adventure; for you, it was a restrictive activity that drained your life force. That over time, evolved into becoming something that was encouraged to be kept to a minimum in the fast-pace corporate environment."

(continued)

Case Study 10.4 (continued)

This journal entry revealed the root causes of the challenge that writing represented a childhood trauma of being controlled. Where the education process and the teachers that taught the subjects I disliked had represented the roles of controlling parents. Where primary needs to appreciate and be appreciated for what I was learning at the time was not a mutual recursive process. It also reflected the impact of my primary capability being Relationship. Wanting to connect and relate to the subjects I was studying through practical experience and dialogue with others. My primary needs and motivations had been historically met through creating and engaging not, just regurgitating information.

Knowing and understanding the origins of my trauma was the key to unlocking the door that revealed the next steps of the transitional journey. What follows is the resourceful purposeful context that my body and mind created in the next journal entry.

A New Context for Writing

It is time to face the daemon in the cupboard that has been shielded from your consciousness. The daemon that carries the not being seen experiences from school. The experiences that feel like a sword had cut off your head from our body. Desensitised the area around the wounding so that it was invisible to the naked eye. Accept that the heart had the power, and knew when it was making itself do something that felt as though was not in service to primary needs. A window into the soul, to know that writing at the time was not reflective of her.

Not like the little girl who played with the donkey and danced with the sheep in the field who got energy from giving energy. Or the small child who saw potential in the smallest glint of an eye the light falling through the trees, illuminating the snowdrops and daffodils at the beginning of spring. Not the little girl who watched the squirrels dance from branch to branch who lifted her face to the sun to acknowledge and embrace its gift of warmth and love.

Where has she been all these years? It is now time to come out and transform coal into gold. Maybe just maybe she can put her toe in the water and stand in the pond with the toad and step into something new. To see a glimmer of hope that writing can be something more than just pain and misery.

What if writing could be liberating, to bring something hidden to the foreground? What if it could be energetic, creative and vibrant, full of colour and life, using words like paint on the end of a brush swirling around the page to create a painting with meaning? To fill herself with energy and excitement just from the thought of writing and put those days of dread and painful misery behind her. To gain a new life force from the words that form and dance as new patterns emerge.

Whilst I had set a purposeful context, transforming my relationship with writing was not going to happen overnight. Healing an embodied trauma and developing a new writing practice was going to require getting access to patterns in unknown self-self dimensions. Questions at the forefront of my mind's eye were, what was I going to have to dismantle and deconstruct? What patterns would I have to interrupt and let go of in order to develop a new relationship with writing?

Table 10.1 Inner knowing framework and first journal entry

Title	Territory of self	Journaling experience	Physical experience	Impact on sense-of-self
Getting started	Rejecting-self	Hard Talking about style From head	Heavy forehead and shoulders Pain at back of eyes	Irritated

Inner Knowing Journaling

An approach that is particularly helpful for uncovering patterns in embodied inquiry is to develop a reflective review of the journaling process. Reflecting on the journaling process is an approach that Turner-Vesselago (2013) also recommends. I find inner-knowing journaling is particularly useful for gaining insight into Sills's (2009) notion of witness consciousness, a process for supporting the Self to see and witness the constructs of the inner world. It is a resourceful approach that can be utilised for drawing awareness to the different qualities in our territories of Self, (central, needy, rejecting) the different Self-relational experiences that we explored in Chap. 4. It is a reflexive process that can be utilised for inquiring into the relational qualities, different types of dialogues and the nature of the relationships that our mind/body holds with itself during the journal writing process. If we are grappling with a challenging transition and transformation process, then understanding how the different territories of Self are informing and showing up in our experiences can be another useful resource.

Table 10.1 is the framework that I developed for capturing inner knowing experiences, along with the first journal entry.

Title Giving our entries a title, is useful for tracking progress over time that provides easy access to referencing and support further review and reflection processes.

Territory of Self This is the context and territory of Self that the writing emanates from, that can be central-self, needy-self or rejecting-self. Reviewing the content of what has been written provides some great clues as to what territory of Self is present.

Case study 10.5 illustrates examples of the different territories of Self that emerged in my journal entries.

> **Case Study 10.5 Needy, Rejecting and Central-Self Examples**
> Needy-Self – *"It is all in my head. What am I going to write? How do I write it? What do I want to say? What am I trying to say? My head feels like a tin can with a tiny hole, trying to catch glimpses of what is inside it, is it sardines? Is it salmon? Is it steam baked treacle pudding? Ah yes, that's it treacle, stuck to the sides of the tin*

(continued)

Case Study 10.5 (continued)

moulded with the uncooked sponge. It does not want to come out. It does not want to be seen. It just wants to be there in the dark on its own in the tin to be left alone. The 'be perfect' driver is pulling me back like a rope noose around my neck. I need everything that goes on paper to be right—told in a way that others will want to see and hear the words. It is for others, so it has got to be right. The context has to be set, the words have to be right, not too sharp, and not too soft they need to be just right. Oh, hang on a sec, that one is not quite shiny enough, lets polish it a bit to make it shine a bit more."

Rejecting-Self – *"Just stop all this nonsense, why are you making this whole process such a big deal? What is the matter with you? You have always found writing hard, what makes you think that it is going to be different this time? Not really sure you are up to this, are you? Just accept that you may not be up to this impossible task. Just accept that writing is hard, and it is not for you. You are just not good enough."*

Central-Self – *"Just write from the heart. Do not worry what fits where, or how it needs to be arranged. Just focus on the heart and speak from the heart. Turn the head off and just be with what arises. Do not worry about what comes up; it will all be relevant. You will find places for it to connect. Be with and in the heart, and it will hold your head's confusion and its need for clarity and structure. Just be with what the heart wants to say. Just keep listening and being with what it says and allow it to guide your whole pathway. Just keep going, and moving one step at a time".*

Journaling Experience   This is a summary of the general sense of the whole journal entry experience. The felt sensations, style of the writing process as it emerges and the prominent features of where it emanates from within the mind/body. A useful question to ask is what was that like?

Physical Experience   Physical experiences relate to the qualities and sensations of the physical body during the writing process. Insightful questions to ask are how is my body feeling? What specific sensations am I experiencing in my body?

Impact on Sense-of-Self   The sense-of-self impact represents the general felt sense qualities at the end of the writing process. These are qualities that have a direct impact on the ways of being of the whole mind/body sense-of-self. A resourceful question to ask is how do I now feel about and within myself?

Case study 10.6 shows how inner knowing journaling provided insight and evidence to support the process of transforming my relationship with writing.

Case Study 10.6 Transforming a Relationship with Writing
While practising inner knowing journaling, through tracking journal entries, I became able to access information that my body held while it was processing the lived experiences of writing. Inner knowing became an embodied process that akin to what Moustakas (1990) describes as Incubation. It was an emerg-

ing generative practice that facilitated insight into embodied knowing that I had been unable to access related to my experiences with writing until that point.

One of the discoveries from the inner knowing practice was that there were connections between the different qualities in self-self dialogue and how I was representing them in my physical and emotional state. For example, when I wrote from the needy or rejecting-self, the process of writing felt physically painful, stressful and draining. Yet on the days when I wrote from the aspect of the central-self, the writing process felt effortless and resourceful. A key insight that illuminated my whole life's experiences with writing had been based on the defensive states of needy and rejecting self-self relationships. In practice, when writing from the territories of the needy and rejecting Self, I was engaging in a judgmental Self-critical state that identified with the trauma of my childhood experiences. And when I wrote from the territory of the central-self, I was relating to my core being. I discovered a new integrated mind/body experience that brought supportive energy and resources to my writing experiences.

Reviewing and reflecting on the inner knowing journal entries, I began to notice the shifts in the felt sense qualities between the different self-territories as they appeared while I was in the process of writing. The outcome was that I became supported by a new context and frame-of-reference for writing. As I discovered the different qualities in the writing process, I began focusing my journaling on topics that were creative and gave me energy. I deliberately stayed away from anything connected to work or education to create a new supportive context to allow my past trauma to heal.

Over four weeks, I learned to calibrate the felt sense qualities of the central-self, let go of my embodied defensive states and develop a new relationship with writing. I knew that I had successfully achieved my outcome by tracking the summary of the inner knowing journal entries. Regardless of whether the writing topic was positive, neutral or negative, my writing emanated from a dialogue with the central-self, and the journaling experiences were consistently based on mind/body congruence. The physical experiences and impact on my sense-of-self transitioned from being emotionally and physically painful into being resourceful.

Table 10.2 shows the last five journal entries that provided the confirming evidence that I had transcended into developing a new self-self relationship with writing.

Inner knowing journaling also had other benefits. As I transcended into embodying a new writing practice, I became able to access what Polanyi (1969) describes as Tacit Knowledge. Knowledge related to my transition practice that had been acquired through action, processed and embodied outside of conscious awareness for over 25 years in working with others in organisations. I replaced the urge to have to know what I was going to write about

(continued)

Case Study 10.6 (continued)

at the outset, to becoming curious and excited as to what I would uncover as my fingers hit the keyboard. This new writing practice formed the basis for the approach that designed and created this textbook.

Table 10.2 "Transcending into a new writing practice" journal entries

Title	Territory of self	Journaling experience	Physical experience	Impact on sense-of-self
Hope	Central-self Dialogue	Fluid Informing Being style From within body	Comfortable Resourceful	Liberated New self-insight
A painful heart	Central-self Dialogue	Fluid Informing Being style From within body	Resourceful	Insightful
A hopeful heart	Central-self Dialogue	Fluid Being style From within body	Cathartic Resourceful	Energy
A pause	Central-self Dialogue	Fluid Emergent Being style From within body	Energy Resourceful Fuzzy Tingling	Congruence Supported Trusted Connected
A sense of connection and calm	Central-self Dialogue	Fluid Emergent Being style From within body	Energy flowing through hands Tingling Resourceful	Heartfelt Joy Connection

Diagnostics

Another way of gaining access to unseen patterns that informs our embodied traits, skills, knowledge and behaviours is through psychometric diagnostics. I find the ones that provide insights into a wide variety of different patterns that support self-inquiry process are the most resourceful. The two that I have found to be the most helpful in supporting leaders to inquire into their transition practices are Launchpad and Voiceprint.

LaunchPad
LaunchPad is an expert psychometric assessment system. It uses an integrated battery of ten established psychometric assessments derived from a range of psycho-

logical and behavioural models, LaunchPad looks for themes and patterns across their outputs to deliver analysis that is both broad and deep. It features a suite of tools for individual reporting, role profiling, team profiling and broader organisational analysis.

Website Link: http://www.launchpadpsychometrics.com

VoicePrint

VoicePrint is an innovative development tool that explores how individuals (and organisations) draw on the resourcefulness of talk. It distinguishes nine different 'voices' or ways of using talk, each of which has a valuable function, but also a dysfunctional counterpart when poorly used. Taking this behavioural focus, and recognising that individual profiles are more diverse and less static than other psychometrics usually portray them, VoicePrint is highly sensitive to individuality and context, making its insights and action points immediately relevant and practical.

Website Link http://www.voiceprint.global

Summary

In this chapter, we have been exploring methods that inform the practice of Self-Inquiry. And, how these different approaches can be utilised to explore patterns in thinking, emotional responses, knowledge, perspectives, assumptions and physical symptoms that form and inform our relationships and behaviours with ourselves and others. In addition, how the practice of embodied self-inquiry can be utilised to gain insight into our self-self relationships that inform known and unknown inner territories. Knowing inner territories can be useful resources for supporting transition leadership practices for ourselves, others and organisations.

An Invitation for Self-Inquiry

If you are interested in incorporating self-inquiry into your transition leadership practice, here are a few questions to consider:

In-Time Inquiry

Stage 1 – What elements are contributing to your current experience?

Experience – what is happening?

Qualities – how are you thinking, feeling, sensing this experience?

Influences – what is informing and contributing to the qualities of the experience?

Past – is there anything familiar about this experience or is it new?

Outcomes – what impact is this experience having on Self, others or the environment?

(continued)

(continued)

> *Stage 2 – Are there any patterns and, if so, what impact are they having?*
>
> *Known* – dimensions that are known and understood
> *New* – anything new, different or surprising
> *Unknown* – elements that raise further questions or that cannot be
> articulated
>
> *Stage 3 – What will your transitional development journey require?*
>
> *Phase 1 Shifting* – what will need to be dismantled and deconstructed?
> *Interrupting Norms* – what familiar aspects will require interrupting?
> *Phase 2 Ending* – what will be required to be disintegrated and
> dissolved?
> *Letting Go* – what known aspects will be required to go?
> *Phase 3 Emerging* – what will require reforming or reconstructing?
> *Creating New* – what new mindsets, behaviours or practices will be
> required?
> *Phase 4* – what will need to be developed?
>
> **Embodied Self-Inquiry**
> In the event of wanting to inquire into embodied knowing:
>
> *Journaling*
>
> 1. What specific aspects do you want to inquire into?
> 2. Why is this important?
> 3. What impact will these have on your transition leadership practice?
> 4. What outcomes are you hoping to achieve?
> 5. How will you know when you have achieved your outcomes?

References

Dewey, J. (1910). *How we think* (1991st ed.). New York: Prometheus Books.

Moustakas, C. (1990). *Heuristic research. Design, methodology, and applications*. Newbury Park: Sage.

Pennebaker, J. W., & Beall, S. K. (1986). Confronting a traumatic event: Toward an understanding of inhibition and disease. *J. Abnorm. Psychol, 95*, 274–281.

Polanyi, M. (1969). *Knowing and being*, Marjorie Grene (Ed.). Chicago: University of Chicago Press.

Richardson, L. (2000). Writing: A method of inquiry. In N. K. Denzin & Y. S. Lincoln (Eds.), *Handbook of qualitative research* (2nd ed.). Thousand Oaks: Sage.

Sills, F. (2009). *Being and becoming*. Berkeley: North Atlantic Books.

Turner-Vesselago, B. (2013). *Writing without a parachute. The art of freefall*. London: Jessica Kingsley Publishers.

Index

© Springer Nature Switzerland AG 2020
C. Hayes, *Transition Leadership*, https://doi.org/10.1007/978-3-030-42787-0

Ingram Content Group UK Ltd.
Milton Keynes UK
UKHW022234120523
421677UK00002B/4